PORTRAIT OF LONDON RIVER

The Tidal Thames from Teddington to the Sea

THE *PORTRAIT* SERIES

71r2

Portrait of
LONDON RIVER

The Tidal Thames from Teddington to the Sea

BASIL E. CRACKNELL

ILLUSTRATED
AND WITH MAPS

ROBERT HALE · LONDON

© *Basil E. Cracknell* 1968
First published in Great Britain 1968

SBN 7091 0300 X

Robert Hale Limited
63 Old Brompton Road
London S.W.7.

40PP

420 793 4163
942.2
CUNNINGHAM

See 942.1

914.22

PRINTED IN GREAT BRITAIN
BY EBENEZER BAYLIS AND SON, LTD.
THE TRINITY PRESS, WORCESTER, AND LONDON

CONTENTS

ILLUSTRATIONS

With the exception of the "muddies" all the illustrations are from photographs taken by the author.

MAPS

I

NOT ONE RIVER BUT THREE

A river is like a living thing. It has a place of birth; it grows from small beginnings to the maturity of the open sea, often marrying another river *en route*; it changes its character with each new environment; it exhibits different moods in different seasons. Its "life force", to borrow Bernard Shaw's description, is a compulsive urge to reach the sea so that the cycle can be repeated once more.

But a tidal river is doubly alive. It changes not only with the seasons, or with the weather, but daily with the tides. There is a regularity of movement here as unchanging as a heart-beat—no wonder the tide is often called the "pulse" of the City of London. Such a tidal river is the subject of our portrait, and there is nothing still-life about it. Old Father Thames below Teddington's tidal barrier is not a quiet sitter. He changes his moods so suddenly; turn a bend and the idyllic peace of Kew Gardens has yielded to urban Mortlake and its great brewery, move on a bridge or two from Kings Reach and you have exchanged the nobility of the Houses of Parliament for the ugliness of the Wapping water-front. However, the author has the advantage over the painter. Whereas the painter can choose only one main aspect of his subject, the author can choose several. I see not one river but three. Above London Bridge the Thames plays essentially a secondary role in relation to the city it has spawned—it is a barrier dividing the city into two halves. I have called this section "The Bridged River" to emphasize its passive role. Londoners are generally most familiar with their river as seen from one of the bridges, embankments, riverside parks or buildings, and these figure prominently in the first part of the book. Of course the bridged river still has an important positive role, especially as a source of recreation. Even in terms of commerce the bridged river handles an annual

tonnage equivalent to that of a major port, but it is completely
overshadowed by the Port of London: the Thames has not yet
come into its own as an artery of commerce.

Below London Bridge the river is king. Here virtually everything that goes on is dominated by the river and its daily régime.
Here are the docks to which above all London owes its position
as one of the world's greatest ports. One of my recurrent themes
in this book is that perhaps that subservience has gone a little too
far, and that it is time the people who live on or near the lower
river were encouraged, and enabled, to enjoy it more. But all this
is a matter of degree. Whatever happens the needs of London the
port must come first, for on the efficient functioning of the port
depends not only the prosperity of the City of London, but also
to a considerable extent the prosperity of the nation as a whole.
In view of its great importance it is curious that most Londoners
know so little about their port—probably only a tiny minority
have seen more of it than can be seen from London or Tower
Bridges. The main reason for this is probably that the docks are
enclosed by high brick walls, and the casual observer is kept out
by policemen stationed at the dock entrances. There is no wander-
ing along the quay picking your way among the fishing nets and
mooring ropes as you can do in any West Country harbour. I
am sure many Londoners are more familiar with the port of Looe
than with the Port of London. The only way to see the port
properly is by water. Therefore in Part II we board a steamer and
take a trip down-river from Tower Pier, through the Royal Docks
and so down to Gravesend the historic gateway to the Thames.

At Gravesend Reach the Thames again changes character. The
stream widens, the banks recede, the river has become an estuary.
We can gain little impression of the fascinating country on either
bank from our steamer, so now we leave her at Gravesend Pier,
the traditional place where the river pilots hand over to the sea
pilots, and we take to the air for a bird's-eye view of some of the
least known parts of London's countryside. We pass over the
beautiful rolling countryside of the Hundred of Hoo on the south
bank, and on the north the remote peninsula of East Tilbury, and
Canvey Island now an urban community of about 20,000 people
but once a little Dutch colony totally isolated from the main-
stream of life. At one time our journey would have ended at the
Nore, for centuries the seaward limit of the Port of London.

But the advent of the super tanker in the last few years has led the Port of London Authority to extend its jurisdiction another twenty-two miles to the Tongue Lightship in the Outer Estuary where the land has almost passed out of sight. So we end our journey at Shoeburyness and Warden Point, looking out towards the stretch of water that navigators of past years regarded as the North Sea, but which has now become a vital part of the Port of London. With ships of ever increasing size, and draught, coming into service it may be that the future of London as a great port may depend upon what happens out there, eighty miles from the little hill by the river where the Romans first established their port and capital city nearly two thousand years ago.

THE RIVER AND THE CITY

"Please to leave the Thames behind you"

Londoners love river-gazing almost as much as they love looking at holes in the ground, and one of the most popular bridges for this sport is Waterloo Bridge. Not only is it one of the most beautiful bridges across the Thames, but very important for the river-gazer, pedestrian and motorist alike, it has low open rails on either side which allow unobstructed views of some of the finest riverscapes to be had in London. Then again it lies between the cities of London and Westminster, about equidistant from their spiritual centres, St Paul's Cathedral and Westminster Abbey. There is indeed no better place from which to enjoy the river, or to ponder the origins of this, one of the greatest cities and ports in the world.

Upstream, beyond the ugly Hungerford Railway Bridge, lies Westminster Bridge, and behind it the towers of Westminster Abbey. This part of the river seems to have had a special significance in Roman times. The land level was higher then than it is today, and the tides reached only about as far as Westminster, whilst today the tides reach as far as Teddington Lock, another twenty miles upstream. There was a sandy island at the mouth of the Tyburn, which joins the Thames at Westminster, and it is probable that the Romans were able to ford the Thames at low tide at this spot. Between Vauxhall Bridge and Waterloo Bridge the river is flowing in a south–north direction, i.e. across its own flood plain. This is a fact of some significance because it means that the river would tend to spread out across the flat flood-plain and would therefore be shallow and more likely to be fordable.

I well remember a particularly successful piece of river-gazing in 1952 when I joined a crowd on Westminster Bridge watching

Lord Noel-Buxton as he walked into the river from St Thomas's Steps at low tide wearing a shirt and flannels. He was attempting to prove that the River Thames had been fordable at low tide in Roman times, and was indeed fordable still, but within a few yards of entering the water he was up to his neck despite his 6 feet 3 inches and in fact he had to swim a good part of the way. (He later wrote a book with the apt title *Westminster Wader*.) I felt rather sorry for him because even if he had been successful he would have proved nothing in relation to the old Roman ford since the Thames today is not the same river as it was then. Not only have there been possibly several changes in the land level, up and down, but the building of embankments, and the narrowing of the river channel, have greatly increased the effect of river scour. However, he was almost certainly right in what he was trying to prove. If one looks at the line of Watling Street, north of the Thames (now the Edgware Road), the first of the Roman roads, it points to where the Houses of Parliament now are, and where the Roman ford would probably have been situated. The orientation of the southern arm of Watling Street through North Kent is a little less convincing however. If it had been directed instead at the City it would have crossed the Thames twice in the course of the river's meander round the Isle of Dogs, and not even the Romans would exhibit this degree of indifference to natural barriers! Thus historical and geological evidence both support the traditional belief that Westminster, rather than London, was the first settlement founded by the Romans.

However, a shallow stretch of water, although it makes a good crossing place, makes a bad port. The Romans must soon have discovered that the Westminster site was quite unsuitable for a port since the larger ships could not come close inshore. A port they must have, for they depended upon rapid communication with the rest of the Empire. They needed a site where the river scoured a deep channel close to the bank, and if possible it had to be in the tidal part of the river because the ebb and flow of the tide provided motive power, an important consideration in days of sail, and indeed today. If possible it should be on the north bank since that would facilitate access to the interior, and it should be so situated that a bridge could be built to communicate with the opposite bank.

The Romans found what they were looking for where the City

of London now stands. If we cross to the other side of Waterloo
Bridge we can look across to St Paul's Cathedral on Ludgate Hill,
some sixty feet above the river. Further east, just out of sight, is
another gravel-topped hill also about sixty feet high, where
Leadenhall Market now stands. The main stream of the river
scours a deep channel close inshore along the concave from
Charing Cross to the Tower. Many of the lanes running down to
the river from the Strand (the name means "river bank" and this
was once the natural bank of the river) drop some thirty feet in a
hundred yards, and many were originally steps leading down to
the water's edge. Essex Street still ends abruptly in a steep flight
of steps. The railway builders were grateful for this natural
feature for it enabled them to bring their lines across the bridges
to the Strand level without large embankments. From our
vantage point on Waterloo Bridge, and still looking towards the
City, we can see Scott's ship the *Discovery*, the sloop *Wellington*
and the two training ships H.M.S. *Chrysanthemum* and H.M.S.
President moored along the Embankment and utilizing the deep
water close inshore. By contrast, on the opposite shore there are
mud flats exposed at every tide, and often lighters and other small
craft will be moored here well away from the fairway. Just round
the bend of the river, at Southwark on the southern bank, there
is a tongue of gravel projecting across the flood plain of the river
towards the City, and this made an ideal landfall for a bridge. So
it came about that all the requirements for a port and capital city
were present. The Romans duly built their new city, protected it
with a great stone wall, threw a wooden bridge across the river . . .
and London was born.

London derives its name from "Londinium". But this is a
latinized word of Celtic origin (the Celtic termination *dun*
suggests a hill fort—probably Cornhill), how then can we be sure
that it was the Romans and not the Celts who founded the city?
The Belgic people who inhabited this part of England when the
Romans arrived tended to avoid the heavily wooded clay lands
such as the Thames Valley. Instead they chose the more open
chalk and gravel lands of the Downs and the Chilterns. Their
capitals were at Verulam (St Albans) and Camulodunum (Col-
chester). When Caesar first set foot in Britain in 55 B.C. the
Belgic people were not much of a trading nation and had little
use for a riverside location. Possibly there were a few minor

Teddington Lock

settlements on the river terrace gravels along the Thames, and Londinium could have been one of these, but they were cut off from the main centres of population by the forests and were insignificant in size. Caesar passed right by the site of London and never mentioned its existence—if indeed it did exist then. It is true that trade with the Continent increased a good deal during the hundred years between Caesar's landing and Vespasian's conquest, and the interesting theory has been advanced that Londinium came into being at this time as a port for Verulam, in which case it would have been situated at the mouth of the River Lea which provided water communication northwards. But whatever development on Thameside actually took place it was certainly on a minor scale. When the Romans returned in earnest in A.D. 43 their first task was to secure adequate communications with their bases in Gaul and with Rome. They remembered how Caesar's ships had been damaged in a storm whilst drawn up on the beaches of Deal, and a safe port was an urgent necessity. The forests of the Thames Valley did not deter them as they could build excellent roads and could clear heavily forested land without great difficulty; thus they were able to concentrate on choosing a site for a good port. They seem to have made a false start at Westminster, but soon corrected this by their choice of London. So it was that Londinium, the isolated clearing in the forest, became London the port and capital city. Perhaps technically speaking it was the Belgii who founded the original settlement, but it was the Romans who made it a city. "The Romans", said G. M. Trevelyan, "left behind them just three things of value: the first . . . was Welsh Christianity; the second was the Roman roads; the third, a by-product of the second, was the traditional importance of certain new city sites, especially that of London."

Roman London had three riverside harbours or "hithes" within the walls. Queenhithe was the most important of these, and it still exists today, although it is seldom noticed because only the avid historian goes down Upper Thames Street (the original river bank and a continuation of the Strand) for pleasure these days—and in any case there is little to see there except an occasional glimpse of the river down a narrow alley between warehouse walls. Then there was Dowgate where the Walbrook, after flowing down the valley between the two hills of Ludgate and Cornhill, entered the Thames just west of where Cannon Street

2

The view from Richmond Hill
Richmond Bridge

Station now stands. The Walbrook was always a great depository of rubbish and it is perhaps fitting that there is now a rubbish-wharf at the point where it joined the Thames. The name Dowgate reminds us that the wall of London once continued along the riverside; the name is commemorated in Dowgate Hill alongside Cannon Street Station. The third harbour of Roman London was Billingsgate, at another gate in the riverside wall.

In addition to the three hithes within the walls there was another just outside the city. This was the estuary of the "Fleet" river, or rather creek, since the river was called the Holborne, and the tidal creek the Fleet. With other keen river-gazers I spent some interesting hours in 1962 watching an old Roman boat about a hundred feet long being lifted from the mud of the Fleet. It was discovered during the construction of the new Blackfriars Underpass. One of the most interesting features was the bronze coin of the Emperor Domitian (A.D. 81–96) which was found in the mast-head step, probably having been put there for luck. It is believed by geologists that there must have been a sharp depression in land level some time during the second century A.D., and the discovery of this ship lends some support to this hypothesis. It is a pity that no permanent site can yet be found for this fascinating if rather cumbersome, piece of history; in the meantime it remains in the custody of the Guildhall Museum hidden from the general public. The Fleet was once crowded with small craft of all kinds, but especially colliers and keel boats from the North-east Coast. Sea-coal Lane, leading off Farringdon Street, dates from at least the sixteenth century and is a reminder of those days, whilst Holborn Viaduct is striking evidence of the steep-sided valley through which the Holborne once flowed. Before the construction of the Viaduct the struggle to get the horses down Snow Hill and up Holborn Hill, "the heavy hill" as it was called, was a notorious hazard. The Fleet was one of the last of Central London's rivers to be buried alive. It suffered this fate in the reign of George II, by which time it had become little more than a stinking open sewer graced with the ignominious title of "Fleet Ditch". Pope had already written its epitaph in his Dunciad:

> Where Fleet Ditch with disemboguing streams
> Rolls the large tribute of dead dogs to the Thames,
> The king of dykes! than whom no sluice of mud
> With deeper sable blots the silver flood.

With its deep flowing river and its several harbours the Port of London continued to flourish whilst the possibly older settlement of Westminster went into decline. When the Romans had built their wooden bridge across the Thames Watling Street was diverted to the City, hence the sharp-angled bend at Marble Arch between Edgware Road and Oxford Street. The later Roman roads, such as Stane Street and Ermine Street, point directly towards London Bridge. The building of the bridge had another very important consequence. Certainly the first stone bridge, completed in A.D. 1209, and probably the earlier wooden bridges also, had many arches and acted as a major barrier to navigation. As a result the ancient quays above the bridge, the Fleet, Dowgate and Queenhithe, although they continued to receive many small vessels and barges, inevitably began to decline in importance, whilst Billingsgate, below the bridge, became the upper limit of navigation for the larger ships. A further consequence of this was that the commercial centre of London grew up around the more easterly of the two hills (Cornhill, where it remains still) since this was nearer the growing harbour of Billingsgate. This downstream migration of shipping and docking facilities, coupled with the growth of barge traffic communicating with wharves upriver, which began a thousand years ago, is the dominant theme in the history of the Port of London and it will reappear many times in this portrait.

If now we walk across to the other side of Waterloo Bridge we have to ask ourselves why it was that in spite of its decline as a crossing place and settlement, it was Westminster and not the City of London that eventually became the seat of government. The explanation is that kings of England have always feared the wealth and affluence of the City of London, far and away the biggest city of the realm and exercising an influence far exceeding that of any other city. Yet they needed the City's support, and could not govern without it, so they sought a compromise. William the Conqueror built the Tower of London on one side of the City, more to overawe its inhabitants than to protect them from outside attack, whilst on the other side the kings and queens of England took up residence at Westminster. From 1066, when Edward the Confessor built his abbey (the "West" minster) on Thorney Island and moved his residence from inside the City to a new Palace alongside the Abbey, Westminster became the political capital of England. The two cities have co-existed in friendly rivalry ever since. There is an old story that when Parliament refused James I a loan, he threatened to move his court to Windsor, whereupon the Lord Mayor, tongue in cheek, replied: "Your City of London will obey accordingly, but she humbly desires that when your Majesty shall remove your Court you would please to leave the Thames behind you."

Even today the friendly rivalry persists in many subtle ways. The Queen, for instance, in her Coronation drive round her capital, had to stop at Temple Bar the traditional entrance to the City of London and declare that she came in peace. The City authorities quietly underlined their territorial boundaries in 1963 by erecting two fine dragons, representing the City of London and removed from the old Coal Exchange when it was demolished in the same year, on the Embankment just west of Temple Lane. Not only the sovereign but also the Prime Minister is careful not to offend the City; the annual visit to the City Fathers at the Guildhall is a first priority in every Prime Minister's calendar. For its part the City has always acknowledged the overlordship of Westminster in the political and judicial realms. Ever since Richard the Lion Heart granted London its Corporation and the office of Lord Mayor came into being in 1193, the newly appointed holder of the office has gone to Westminster where he makes his final declaration of office before the Lord Chief Justice, a custom which survives today as the Lord Mayor's Show. He is accompanied by liveried watermen as befits the holder of the title Admiral of the Port of London. These ancient traditions span a thousand years of history, and probably their origins have been forgotten by most people, but long may they survive to bring colour and a touch of magic to our daily lives.

London the Port, and Westminster the seat of Government, grew side by side, and soon the two had coalesced to form one metropolitan area which grew so fast that it far outstripped all the other cities of Britain and indeed of the world. Even the rapid growth of the industrial North and Midlands during and after the Industrial Revolution did not shift the centre of gravity from London. The city remained the nexus for the country's communications system. Like the Roman roads nearly two thousand years before, all the main railways had their termini in London. There was not a single main-line railway that passed right through the city, or even by-passed it. The capital's dominance was absolute. Even as early as 1801 London's population had almost reached the million mark, and it had become a metropolitan area of such a size that for a long time the world had nothing to match it.

How did it come about that such a mighty city could have been spawned by such a small country, and on such a relatively insignificant river? Most Londoners must have asked themselves that question. For an answer we must look at London's geographical position in relation not only to Britain but to the world as a whole, and particularly to Europe. In relation to Britain the Thames provides a deep penetration into the heart of the country, and a far safer anchorage than any coastal location could afford. You have to go to the Humber or to the Solent before you find anything comparable, and neither has as good access to the interior. In relation to Europe the Thames enters the North Sea immediately opposite one of the most densely populated parts of Europe which has excellent communications with Central Europe, particularly along the Rhine. One might ask why one of the European ports such as Rotterdam or Antwerp, did not outgrow London since they have the advantage of actually being situated on the mainland. The reason is that London had one great advantage. At times when Europe was convulsed with wars and revolutions London always had a stable government, and it was safe. Thus London became the great trading and financial entrepôt for Europe and the world. London also benefited from its position as the centre of a world-wide Empire and trading community, whilst the sharing of a common language and origins with the people of North America stimulated the growth of trade between the Old World and the New. These are the fundamental geographical reasons underlying London's growth to pre-eminence as a world port, but I am not so foolish as to suggest that they are sufficient explanation in themselves; men like Drake, Raleigh, Hudson and Cook, had something to do with it as well.

Since the Second World War the factors of geographical location which once worked to London's advantage have begun to work the other way. London lies on a relatively small island. It was convenient in times past for cargoes to be shipped to London from all parts of the world and then redistributed to other ports in Europe and elsewhere—this was called the "entrepôt" trade of

London. But with the steadily increasing size of ships now coming into service for certain commodities, notably oil and grain, London's island location has become a disadvantage because it limits the available market for these commodities. Thus when a tanker or bulk grain ship arrives at Rotterdam the products can be rapidly distributed all over Europe by road, rail or barge, but if such a vessel arrives at London it can only be distributed in Europe if it is put back into a ship again. These factors help to explain the tremendous growth in the European ports of Rotterdam (or Europoort its new out-port), Antwerp and Amsterdam, since the war.

Here is a vital challenge to London as a port, and indeed to Britain's prosperity as a trading nation. Furthermore if Britain fails to get into the Common Market it may be that the European market, which at present takes more than half our exports, may be progressively denied to us. Of course the Port of London Authority is fully alive to the situation, and they are doing all they can to ensure that London retains its share of world trade. They are deepening the approach channels, building ultra-modern roll on-roll off terminals and a huge bulk grain silo at Tilbury, and encouraging the development of container traffic. Their underlying philosophy is that London lies within the "Golden Triangle" which is formed by Birmingham, Paris and the Ruhr, and which includes the most important industrial activity in Northern Europe, and that the relationship between the great ports within the triangle need not always be competitive but should sometimes be complementary. For example a huge super tanker might call first at Rotterdam, and then, after unloading part of its cargo of oil so that it sits higher in the water, could come across to London to unload the rest. This is already happening and it is an example of co-operation rather than competition. We must be thankful that the Port of London Authority are tackling the problem so determinedly. For let us make no mistake, the whole future of London as one of the world's great ports is at stake. If a sense of urgency creeps into this portrait of the Tidal Thames, especially in the parts dealing with the Port, I make no apology. The challenge is as real today as it was in 1800 when London either had to build enclosed docks or see its trade pass to a port that would.

PART ONE

THE BRIDGED RIVER

TO GOD AND THE BRIDGE

London Bridge has played an almost legendary role in the capital's history. At times it has been treated almost with veneration; the Corporation of London has some old deeds of grants of land "To God and the Bridge". This attitude is no accident, for the bridge remained the only crossing of the river for the first 1,700 years of London's existence. It was the bridge which had a major influence on where the city was sited, the direction in which it grew and the pace of its growth. The history of the bridge is a key to the history of London itself.

Hilaire Belloc said that London River ended at London Bridge. The river that truly gave greatness to London, and earned the right to be called by its name, lay below the bridge. Even in Roman times the bridge, with its many arches, must have been a barrier to navigation. Because of this they must have chosen the site with the greatest care. But what is so strange is that despite several important changes in land level, with all the changes in topography these must have brought in their train, London Bridge has remained just where the Romans put it. The explanation can only be that once the City had been established it could not be moved, so the bridge simply had to be rebuilt where it was despite the difficulties. And of course once this decision had been taken it determined the future growth of the city, for building another bridge was too great a task to be embarked upon until the rapid growth in population made this essential.

We know almost nothing about the Roman bridge, or rather bridges, for there must surely have been many as they were built of wood and had only a limited span of life. The first real evidence of the existence of the Roman bridges came to light in 1834 when some stout oak piles were dredged from the river near the site of the old bridge; they were found to have shoes of a hard iron that

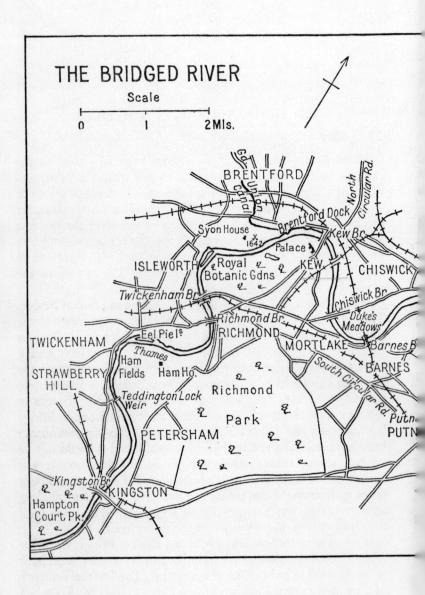

THE BRIDGED RIVER

Scale

0   1   2 Mls.

BRENTFORD

Grand Junction Canal

Brentford Dock

North Circular Rd.

Kew Br.

Syon House
×
1642

Palace

CHISWICK

ISLEWORTH

Royal
Botanic Gdns

KEW

Twickenham Br.

Chiswick Br.

Duke's
Meadows

Richmond Br.

RICHMOND

MORTLAKE

Barnes B

TWICKENHAM

Eel Pie Is.

BARNES

Ham
Fields

Thames

Ham Ho.

South Circular Rd.

STRAWBERRY
HILL

Richmond

Putn

Teddington Lock
Weir

Park

PUTN

PETERSHAM

Kingston Br.

KINGSTON

Hampton
Court Pk.

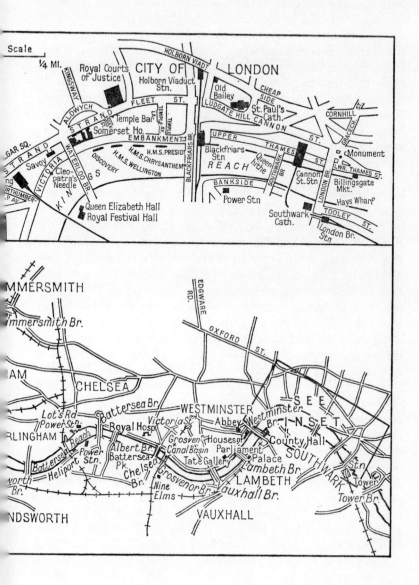

only the Romans could have made. Some years before, when the old medieval bridge was being demolished, Roman coins were dredged up in chronological order covering the whole period of the Roman occupation. What happened during the dark ages following the Roman withdrawal is pure conjecture but it seems likely that the bridge was kept in being for the Venerable Bede around A.D. 730 described London as: "The mart of many nations resorting to it by sea and land." The first direct mention of the bridge in written records does not come until the time of Athelwold, Bishop of Winchester, who died in A.D. 984. This is a reference in the *Codex Diplomaticus* to a woman being punished for witchcraft by drowning ". . . at London Bridge". There are several other mentions of the bridge in Anglo-Saxon writings, especially the Anglo-Saxon *Chronicle*, but the most interesting by far is the account in the *Olaf Sagas* of the destruction of the bridge by King Olaf. He was attacking London, held by the Anglo-Saxons, with a fleet of Danish ships, and found his way blocked by London Bridge on which the defenders were massed. First he built protective decking over his ships, to prevent the rowers from being hurt by missiles thrown from the bridge above, and then he moved forward to the attack. He rowed his ships under the bridge, attached ropes to the piles on which the bridge was supported, and with the help of the tide managed to loosen them so much that the bridge, together with the many soldiers and great heaps of stones which were on it, collapsed into the river. This incident is interesting, not only because it is possibly the origin of the old nursery rhyme "London Bridge is Falling Down", but because it shows how comparatively light a structure the bridge must have been, even though the record describes it as ". . . so broad that two waggons could pass each other upon it". As to the nursery rhyme theory it is interesting that the Norse poet Ottar Svarte wrote a poem which begins: "London Bridge is broken down, Gold is won and bright renown." If I may be slightly facetious for a moment, I noticed when passing under London Bridge recently that it has a definite list to one side, a comparison between the stonework and the water-line shows that the downstream side is about nine inches lower in the water than the upstream. Perhaps it does not matter much because London Bridge is being demolished at the time of writing and will be pulled down long before it falls down!

Another interesting feature of the Olaf Saga description is that the bridge obviously had an important role in defending the river, and the city, from waterborne attack. The *Sagas* record that on the bridge were built towers and wooden parapets ". . . in the direction of the river". In the time of Canute, and on several occasions subsequently, the bridge was the main defence against attack from the river. Even as late as the fourteenth century Gravesend further downstream was burned and destroyed by a French fleet coming up the Estuary, and the exploits of the Dutch fleet in 1677 are a vivid reminder that a river is not only a highway for commerce but a ready-made line of attack for the invader.

Some time during the Norman period it seems that the period of land-emergence which followed the first-century depression came to an end, and was succeeded by a subsidence of the land which has continued slowly ever since. The history of these changes in land level is only slowly being pieced together and is still imperfectly understood. Dramatic new evidence came to light when the South Denes Power Station was being built on a sand spit at Great Yarmouth in the 1950s. It was this, together with a great deal of supporting geological and historical research, which enabled a team of experts to prove that the Norfolk Broads were not natural at all, but were simply flooded peat excavations which had been dry at the time of working, and which had gradually become flooded as the land sank. The deep borings for the power station foundations enabled this same team to put forward the hypothesis that the first-century depression was followed by a rise in the land level until some time during the Norman period, when the process was reversed. It is well known that there is a slow downward tilting of the whole of South-east England, and a corresponding upward movement of the North-western parts of Britain. The movement is very small, perhaps a foot every century, but over a long period of time it is of the greatest significance in all the low-lying coastal areas.

If these hypotheses are correct they may help us to understand the history of the bridge. For instance it seems that until the Norman period a light timber structure may have been adequate, but with the subsidence of the Norman period the river's scour would be increased and the bridge would be in jeopardy. It is tempting to look for evidence, in the historical records, of the bridge needing more repairs, and these can readily be found. For instance in 1091 there was such a high tide that the whole bridge was swept away.[1] In 1136 there was a complete rebuilding of the bridge in elm, but this did not last long, and only forty years later it was decided to rebuild the bridge in stone. In themselves these incidents do not prove that the bridge was subject to any more stress in the Norman period than it was before, simply because comparable records do not exist for the earlier period. But if we cannot fairly infer anything in the comparative sense at least they indicate that by 1176 the situation had become so bad that a stone bridge was the only solution.

It was decided to build the new bridge a little to the east of the timber one, and the money was raised by a tax on wool—hence the saying that London Bridge was built on woolpacks. It was intended that the cost of maintaining the bridge would be met from rents received from the tenants of the houses built on the bridge; however, Henry III, casting round for a convenient source of revenue in 1249, promptly confiscated the rents and there was no money to pay for the upkeep of the bridge. As a result special taxes had to be levied for this purpose, with important consequences for the development of the Thames Estuary region as we shall see later.

The new stone bridge, Old London Bridge, dominated the River Thames for the next 550 years. During the whole of that time there was no other bridge across the Thames below Kingston. The importance of this, in focusing all movement across the river into one place, can hardly be exaggerated. It is small wonder that the City authorities used all their powerful influence, and for a long time with complete success, to ensure that no other bridges were built. As a result the City of London became tightly packed in and around the bridgehead and along the riverside itself. On the south bank there was some development at right angles to the river fanning out from the bridgehead at Southwark, but otherwise there was nothing except a thin strip of development along the river bank. For 550 years Old London Bridge virtually dictated the shape and speed of London's growth, until ultimately the

[1] Only six years later, according to the Anglo-Saxon Chronicle, the bridge (presumably newly rebuilt after the 1091 destruction) was "nearly washed away".

City threatened to die of apoplexy and the monopoly was broken.

The last of the twenty arches and nineteen piers of the new stone bridge were completed in 1209, thirty-three years after the work had started. The new bridge was sited slightly to the east of the old so that the latter would remain in use whilst the new one was being built. The arches were pointed and irregular in size, and in the centre was a wooden drawbridge which served the double purpose of protecting the City from attack across the bridge, and enabling tall ships to pass through into the upper river. The most remarkable feature of the bridge, however, was of course the street of houses and shops which was built on it as soon as the structure was completed. Although the bridge was only twenty feet wide, somehow they managed to build three-storey timber-framed houses on it whilst still preserving a passageway below for vehicles and pedestrians. There were gaps in the line of buildings to enable the larger vehicles to pass on the bridge, but woe betide any pedestrian who got caught between the wheels! It was thanks to these gaps that only a small part of the bridge was destroyed during the Great Fire of 1666. The houses were occupied by people of wealth until the latter days when it became unfashionable to live on the bridge and the houses were eventually removed.

The building of the bridge inevitably affected the wharves and docks up-river which declined in importance. Raising the draw-bridge was a slow business, and ships generally stayed at Billings-gate if they could. In fact the tower supporting the drawbridge had become so weak by 1480 that it was decided not to open the drawbridge again unless the City were threatened by attack. This indeed happened during Sir Thomas Wyatt's rebellion in 1554, but then the bridge authorities decided that it was safer to destroy the wooden drawbridge so that it could not be raised. Wyatt was forced to make the long detour via Kingston Bridge and by the time he arrived at the City along the north bank he had lost most of his followers and the rebellion was over. The disused drawbridge was final recognition of the fact that henceforth the main part of the Port of London would lie below the bridge.

Elizabethan London must have been one of the most compact and crowded cities in the world. In 1550, according to Wyn-gaerde's map, the city was still virtually encompassed by the old

Roman wall. Here and there development had taken place outside
the wall, and there was a thin line of houses stretching as far as
Westminster. On the south bank there was nothing but fields
and market gardens all the way along the river bank from
Southwark to Lambeth. However, London was about to burst out
of its shell. The population was growing, trade was expanding as
new territories were discovered and colonized, and much new
wealth was flowing into the country. Inevitably the pressure for
more spacious living grew rapidly. Innovations in transport
speeded the trend. In 1565 the hackney coach brought a new
mobility, much to the annoyance of the watermen who feared a
threat to their livelihood. John Taylor, the Elizabethan poet, gave
voice to their fears:

> Carrouches, coaches, jades and Flanders mares,
> Do rob us of our shares, our wares, our fares,
> Against the ground we stand and knock our heels,
> Whilst all our profit runs away on wheels.

Even the introduction of the sedan chair in 1634 facilitated
short distance journeys within the crowded city. Mansions began
to spring up all along the riverside as far as Chelsea, whilst even
on the south bank development was taking place alongside the
river.

Meanwhile London Bridge had taken on a new and unusual
role. In 1580 the first water mill was installed between one of the
arches on the north end for the pumping of water to supply
the city. It was so successful that another was installed in 1582,
and in 1599 a third was installed, this time on the south end, for
the grinding of corn. Eventually most of the arches were used for
driving water mills. The original water contractors were given a
contract lasting 500 years which proved awkward when the
bridge was demolished; the heirs still receive compensation from
the Metropolitan water Board, and will continue to do so for a
good many years yet. The successful operation of these water
mills depended upon the bridge acting like a weir, that is the water
had to be higher on one side than on the other. The design of the
bridge, with its many arches each protected by huge "starlings"
or buttresses of stone and rubble sheathed in piles of timber,
ensured that the bridge would sufficiently impede the flow to give
a head of water. It has been estimated that the flow was reduced

Strand on the Green
Chelsea's houseboat Village

by 25 per cent as a result of the bridge. The freezing of the Thames above London Bridge, which gave rise to the famous Frost Fairs, was due to the sluggishness of the water caused by the obstruction of the bridge. The Great Frost Fair of 1684 lasted nearly three months and whole oxen were roasted on the ice; a printing press made a lucrative business printing people's names "on the ice of the River Thames". Thanks to the removal of Old London Bridge there are unlikely ever again to be any Frost Fairs on the Thames.

The erection of the water mills added to the barrier effect of the bridge itself, and helped to channel the tidal flow into the two or three open arches in the centre. Here the current ran so swiftly that watermen would speak of "shooting the bridge". A class of watermen even came into existence called "bridge shooters". The saying arose that wise men walked over London Bridge and only fools went under it. Cardinal Wolsey certainly acted on this maxim—whenever he had to go to Greenwich he always landed at the Three Cranes, made his way along Thames Street, and reboarded the boat below the bridge. There was another saying that you could never cross London Bridge without seeing a white horse. The passage of the arches had to be undertaken with care, and vessels were in the habit of queuing up whilst those ahead went through; vessels seldom passed through at high tide since the tops of the timber starlings were then submerged and out of sight. The early part of the flood was the best time to make the passage as the current was then at its least.

The Plague of 1665, and the Great Fire a year later, led to the rapid outward expansion of London because it was realized that overcrowding had to be reduced if such calamities were to be avoided in the future. So it was that the expansion of London, which had really started as a result of the Civil War, gained greatly in momentum and rapid development took place along both banks of the river. Inevitably there began to be severe congestion and delays at the bottle-neck Old London Bridge. Yet the City authorities were still successfully resisting any attempt to build new bridges across the Thames. Even before the Great Fire, in 1664, there had been a proposal to build a bridge across the Thames between Lambeth and Westminster, but the City Fathers had sent delegates to Charles II with an offer of a loan of £100,000 if he would oppose the scheme and this he duly did. It was almost

3

another century before this bridge was eventually built and the monopoly of London Bridge was broken.

Even the powerful opposition of the City could not forever defy the elementary facts of geography. Already by 1745 London had become distorted into a long sausage-shaped city strung out along the river with very little development inland. The river itself was still the main avenue of communication between one part of the city and another, and for many people was the means by which they travelled to their work. The first sign of a break in the City's monopoly was the construction of a crude wooden toll bridge at Putney in 1729, and this was followed shortly afterwards by the building of Westminster Bridge, completed in 1750. It was on this bridge, of course, and not on the present one, that Wordsworth wrote his memorable lines: "Earth has not anything to show more fair . . ." Kew Bridge followed quickly after in 1758. Perhaps it was this challenge to their control of the cross-river traffic that led the City authorities in 1757 to remove all the buildings from London Bridge so as to increase the flow of traffic across the bridge. Two years later the centre arches were removed and replaced by one larger arch. However, this only increased the scour of the river, since it had the effect of breaching a dam, and for the next fifty years heavy expenditure was incurred in maintaining the bridge intact. Even the gates of the old City, removed in 1766 when the old Roman Wall was finally demolished, were thrown into the bed of the river by the piers of the old bridge in a desperate attempt to reduce the erosion. The waterworks were removed in 1822, but nothing now could save the old bridge, it would have to come down. The new bridge was begun in 1825, about 180 feet to the west of the old one, and it was opened six years later. London Bridge had fallen down—it was the end of an era.

How many Londoners have wondered, as I did once, why the Monument was built in such an out-of-the-way spot which seems altogether unworthy a site for such an edifice? The explanation is that when it was built it lay at the northern end of Old London Bridge. The old bridge led directly to Fish Hill and so to Gracechurch Street; when the new bridge was built Gracechurch Street had to be diverted and became the main approach road, leaving Fish Hill and the Monument in a backwater. Even more poignant is the fate that befell Wren's lovely church of St Magnus

Martyr which lay at the foot of Fish Hill, to give a Christian greeting, as it were, to travellers as they stepped off the bridge. Further to assist the traveller Wren built a fine clock overhanging the road, and the pavement passed through the very base of the tower. But when the New Fresh Wharf was being built in the 1920s they needed the maximum possible wharf-side space and so St Magnus Martyr was walled in by a new warehouse many storey's high. The old church is still there, grimy and neglected and smelling of fish from broken fish boxes scattered about outside; its magnificent clock is now a mockery, and where the people once jostled and carriages rumbled across the bridge, there is only a tiny sunless courtyard complete with a few sad stones from the old bridge. When Adelaide House was being built they discovered the first two arches of Old London Bridge; an attempt was made to raise the few thousand pounds needed to preserve them, but there was no response and the arches were demolished. What a sad epitaph to the story of Old London Bridge

During the hundred years preceding the rebuilding of London Bridge London had changed almost out of recognition. The population had vastly increased, metalled roads had transformed the communication network, and canals, and later railways and steamships, were bringing a new mobility within the reach of the ordinary man. People were on the move. It was apparent to all that the two bridges across the Thames in London were utterly inadequate for the changing circumstances. So began the first great period of bridge-building. New bridges followed each other in quick succession. In 1769 Blackfriars Bridge, originally christened Pitt Bridge, was built, sounding the death knell to Wren's ambitious plans for the Fleet River. Blackfriars Bridge was built by the City authorities out of tolls received from London Bridge; now that their monopoly had been broken their attitude had changed and they were anxious to ensure that the City's cross-river facilities were as good as possible. Blackfriars was followed two years later by Battersea's high wooden bridge, immortalized in Whistler's "Nocturne"; and by Richmond Bridge in 1777, the subject of one of Turner's less dramatic but no less beautiful paintings and now the oldest bridge below Teddington Lock. Paine's ten-arched Kew Bridge came in 1789. The end of the Napoleonic Wars saw a new burst of activity in bridge-building. In 1816 came Vauxhall Bridge, the first to be built of

iron and often known as the Regents Bridge as it was opened by
the Regent; in 1817 Rennie's Waterloo Bridge, which began life
as the Strand Bridge and was renamed in a wave of patriotic
fervour; in 1819 Southwark, another iron bridge designed to
obtain the maximum span possible; and in 1827 the suspension
bridge at Hammersmith.

All these bridges were of course situated on the up-river side
of London Bridge. But during the eighteenth and nineteenth
centuries the Port of London had been rapidly growing and the
City had spread out eastwards to embrace the docks. Before the
days of motor-cars and buses people generally had to live as near
as possible to their place of employment; thus Dockland became
densely populated and the problem of cross-river communication
became ever more pressing. Clearly bridges of the traditional
kind were out of the question as they would interfere with
navigation on the river. Attention therefore turned to possible
alternatives.

The first was of course tunnels. As early as 1798 an attempt
had been made to drive a tunnel under the River Thames between
Gravesend and Tilbury, but it had to be abandoned five years
later because of geological and financial difficulties. Another
unsuccessful attempt was made a few years later when Richard
Trevethick had to abandon the tunnel for pedestrians he was
building between Limehouse and Rotherhithe after he had
almost completed it. The next attempt was in 1824 when Brunel
began to build a tunnel of twin arches joining Wapping and
Rotherhithe using a new technique he had invented after studying
the boring method of the shipworm *Teredo Navalis*. Despite
tremendous difficulties (the Thames broke through nearly a dozen
times) during which the tunnel earned the nickname "The Great
Bore", it was completed in 1843. Incredibly enough, however, the
spiral ramps planned by Brunel to provide wheeled access were
never built, so that the tunnel could only be used by pedestrians
and was a financial failure. Ultimately it was taken over by the
East London Railway Company, in 1866, and was incorporated
into the Underground system in 1869. It has had the unusual
distinction of being used sometimes at night by steam trains.

After Brunel's tunnel, and thanks particularly to his pioneer-
ing work in devising new techniques, the building of tunnels
became commonplace, especially for the new underground

trains, and today there are many tunnels crossing the river, including two pedestrian subways at Greenwich and Woolwich. There was once a pedestrian subway by the Tower of London which has a particular place in railway history since it was the first to be built using the true "tube" system; when Tower Bridge was built it was closed to pedestrians and now carries pressure mains. The new Dartford–Purfleet tunnel was opened a short time ago, and a new road tunnel at Blackwall, parallel with the existing one, is almost completed. A new tunnel is planned to link the South Circular Road and the North Circular Road and to serve the new town of Thamesmead; this will pass under the Thames in the vicinity of Woolwich and will replace the vehicle ferry there.

Apart from tunnels, the second alternative to bridges of the usual kind was the high-level bridge, or the bridge that opened to allow the passage of vessels. Both ideas were much canvassed. In the early 1800s Captain Brown, a manufacturer of heavy chains, proposed the building of a high-level suspension bridge across the river, but the idea was never taken up, presumably because of the prohibitive cost of building the huge approach ramps. Some time before that Telford had proposed a high level fixed bridge in iron, but again the idea was rejected because of the space needed for the approach roads. The lift-bridge seemed a far more promising idea. The Port of London Authority have in their possession a beautiful print illustrating a proposal by George Dance, Clerk of the City Works, as far back as 1800, for London Bridge to be rebuilt as twin bridges parallel to each other, each with a drawbridge across the centre span to allow the passage of vessels; the object of having twin bridges was that traffic could be diverted over the second bridge whilst the drawbridge of the first was being raised and vice versa ... an early example of tidal flow traffic technique! However, Dance was eighty-five years ahead of his time, and London had to wait until 1886 before the Tower Bridge was built. Tower Bridge was not the first drawbridge in London's history since old London Bridge had a drawbridge until the sixteenth century.

As Londoners watched the new Tower Bridge going up in the late 1880s, they must have despaired. *Country Life* recently published a photograph taken at the time. It shows a horribly ugly and gaunt steel frame, massive in scale (the designers were determined that the Tay Bridge disaster would not be repeated on the Thames), rising above the river like some colossal monument to a new steel age. But gradually the picture was transformed before their eyes. The steel was covered by a skin of brickwork, and clothed with a facing of granite, and a new shape came into being—a neo-medieval structure as far removed from the new Steel Age as could be imagined. For this they had the War Office to thank. With a concern for topography which one seldom associates with that body, the War Office had insisted that the new bridge should harmonize with the Tower of London. Sir Horace Jones, one of the designers, would have taken this injunction even further than was intended; he proposed to raise and lower the bascules by means of huge chains, like the drawbridge of a Crusader's castle. After his death in 1887, however, wiser counsels prevailed and the idea of chains was abandoned. Each bascule weighs 1,100 tons, and the machinery for operating them is housed in the base of each tower; when lowered the bascules are held in position by four huge bolts that are operated hydraulically. Despite their great weight the bascules are raised and lowered in the remarkably short time of three minutes. Usually they are not raised to their full height; this honour is only given to the City's most distinguished visitors, the most recent occasion being the visit of Sir Francis Chichester on his return from his voyage round the world. The bane of the bridge-master's life is the vessel with a hinged mast that makes Tower Bridge open and then steps its mast to pass under London Bridge!

The bridge-master has a staff of some eighty men to assist him in operating the bridge, and alongside the bridge there is always a tug on duty in case any shipping should get into difficulties while approaching or passing through the bridge. Vessels wishing to have the bridge opened give one long and three short blasts on their sirens (this is the morse signal for "B", presumably for "Bridge"), and they hoist a black ball and pennant at the forestay. In the case of vessels coming upstream a telephone message is sent from Cherry Garden Pier advising the bridge-master that the vessel is approaching, but in the case of vessels coming downstream the watchman on the bridge keeps a constant lookout. The bridge is equipped with four semaphore signals which look exactly like railway signals. By Act of Parliament river traffic takes absolute precedence over road traffic. The footbridges across the top have not been used since before the First World War, partly because of the difficulty of policing them, and partly because they had in any case fallen into disuse as people preferred to wait the few minutes for the bascules to be raised and lowered. The bascules are raised up to ten times a day, usually during the period just before high water. There have been rumours recently that Tower Bridge will be demolished but I am informed by the City Engineer of the Corporation of London that in fact there are no plans to demolish the bridge. However, in view of the increasing volume of cross-river traffic using this bridge a new tunnel has been proposed so that vehicular traffic can by-pass the bridge. In this case the bridge would probably remain with its two bascules permanently raised—an honourable retirement for what has become a world-wide symbol of London.

The rebuilding of London Bridge in 1825–31 signalled the beginning of the period of reconstruction of London's major bridges. In the hundred years following 1825 many new bridges were built, but apart from Wandsworth Bridge (opened in 1873 and rebuilt in 1936) only the four suspension bridges, Hammersmith (built in 1827, the first suspension bridge over the Thames, and rebuilt in 1887), Lambeth (1862—rebuilt in traditional style in 1932), Chelsea (1858) and Albert (1873) were built on entirely new sites, the others were all reconstructions of older bridges. Not only was this rebuilding process initiated chronologically by the rebuilding of London Bridge but it was in a very real sense a consequence of it. For the removal of Old London Bridge had a major effect upon the tidal régime of the upper river. As soon as the "weir" was removed the volume of water passing up and down the river considerably increased, the scour was greater, and it was not many years before the foundations of the bridges further up-river were being undermined. Westminster Bridge was the first to be seriously affected and it had to be pulled down and replaced by the present one in 1862. Almost at the same time Blackfriars Bridge was demolished and the new one, the widest bridge over the Thames, was erected in 1869. In 1882 the increased scour began to expose the foundations of Waterloo Bridge. Repairs were made, but these were ineffective. By 1924 the condition of the bridge had deteriorated so much that a temporary one had to be built alongside the old one and a one-way traffic system installed. The new bridge was built during the 1939–45 War. It is the first concrete bridge to be built across the Thames and it is to the flexibility in design that this material makes possible that Waterloo Bridge owes its wonderfully slim and shapely lines. Furthermore it was built in a period of austerity and is therefore free from embellishments of architectural detail—hence its clean uncluttered appearance. After Blackfriars came in quick succession Putney (1886), designed by Sir Joseph Bazalgette who we shall meet in the next chapter as the designer of London's great embankments, Hammersmith (1887), Battersea (1890), Kew (1904), and Vauxhall in 1906. Vauxhall Bridge is particularly interesting because each of the four stone piers on which the steel arches rest is embellished with a pair of statues, one statue facing upstream, and the other downstream. These statues symbolize in a neat way the cultural boundary which Vauxhall represents. Upstream is an ugly industrial clutter, and the statues on this side represent Engineering, Pottery, Architecture and Agriculture, whereas on the downstream side, looking towards the Tate Gallery, the Houses of Parliament and County Hall, are statues representing Fine Arts, Local Government, Science and Education. It is a pity, though, that the millions who cross the bridge never see the statues. After the First World War came Southwark, the narrowest and least used of London's bridges (1921), Lambeth (1932), Twickenham, Chiswick and Chelsea in 1937, and Wandsworth in 1940. By 1945 all London's major bridges had been rebuilt and the rebuilt London Bridge had already become the oldest of the main Thames bridges.

One would like to forget the railway bridges of London because they are ugly eyesores that detract from the architectural landscape and add nothing of value to it. Holborn, in particular, kills what should be a fine view downstream from Blackfriars, and Charing Cross has already interrupted our musings from Waterloo Bridge on the upstream side. Charing Cross railway bridge, built in 1862, is the more regrettable still because it replaced Brunel's elegant Hungerford suspension footbridge and the two Italianate towers from which the central span of 676 feet was suspended. Some of the chains eventually found their way to Bristol where they were used in the building of the Clifton Suspension Bridge, whilst the original brick pillars for Brunel's bridge were utilized as supports for the new railway bridge.

Cannon Street and Victoria bridges were built during this mid-Victorian period which was aesthetically a disaster so far as the Thames in London is concerned.

There are today no less than twenty-eight bridges, including the railway bridges, across the Thames between Teddington and Tower Bridge. Yet still the traffic problems of London become more and more acute. Anyone who has been caught in a rush-hour traffic jam at one of the bridge-heads, or tunnel entrances, will agree that the river crossings are among the most serious of London's traffic problems. The number of cars is certain to increase steadily in the years ahead, and there can be no possible solution to the traffic problems presented by the Thames without more tunnels and more bridges. Several such bridges are already being planned. For instance a number of existing bridges will be rebuilt to accommodate increased traffic, and a new bridge is planned to link the westerly arms of the North and South Circular roads at Barnes, whilst another is planned for the West Cross Route at Chelsea. As to the railway bridges we have heard little since the war of Sir Patrick Abercrombie's bold scheme for bringing the main railway lines into central London through tunnels, allowing the bridges to be demolished, and I understand from the Chief Civil Engineer of British Railways that there are no plans at present for the demolition of any railway bridges.

What will the new bridges look like? There is a ferment of ideas in architectural circles which is most exciting and encouraging. Just in recent months a design was published containing a proposal for a new bridge to replace the Hungerford Railway Bridge. This has been conceived with the needs of pedestrians in mind as much as motorists; the bridge would have several layers of shops and raised walkways with the vehicles passing underneath. Lord Holford's design for the new London Bridge, work on which has already been started, makes provision for the roadway to be covered eventually (say in fifteen years' time) by a high-level pedestrian walkway with access by conveyors. It is only one step forward from this to the provision of shops, and even to the building of exclusive apartments . . . and we are back at Old London Bridge. The second rebuilding of London Bridge, already begun, will inaugurate the third generation of London's main bridges. What a great opportunity there is here to give London a new look—or rather the look it lost two centuries ago when Old London Bridge was shorn of its buildings. Perhaps we shall see bridges with several decks, the lower one, or ones, for vehicles, and the upper for pedestrians alone, with cafés, shops, restaurants, art galleries, and viewing balconies. In this way the river could be woven more intimately into the fabric of the city, and the north bank could be knitted to the south more effectively than in any other way. Perhaps Norden's description of London Bridge in the sixteenth century may be equally applicable to its successor in the twentieth: " . . . adorned with sumptuous buildings, and statlie and beautiful houses on either side, inhabited by wealthy citizens and furnished with all manner of trades comparable in itselfe to a little Citie."[1]

[1] Quoted from *London's Riverside: Past, Present and Future* by Eric de Maré, 1958, page 88.

4

THE RIVER EMBANKED

"A Commodious Key"

Even the most unseeing of river-gazers must be aware of the way the River Thames changes its character twice a day with the rise and fall of the tide. Knowing how the tides work is the key to understanding so much about what happens on the tideway that we will conduct a little experiment as an alternative to a tiresome technical explanation. First we take a seven-foot plank of wood, and we build a little mast on it to which we attach a flag—purely so that we can identify it among all the other flotsam and jetsam in the river. We place our primitive craft in the lower part of the river just as the tide begins to flow. We follow it as the tide carries it up-river, and five hours later, when the tide turns again, it will have been carried fourteen or fifteen miles up the river. With the ebbing tide it will be carried back again for seven hours, until the cycle is repeated. Gradually the plank will be carried further down-river, but the process may take five or six weeks. The tide is a great source of motive power for small vessels, and it was by using it that dumb barges (i.e. those without any engines) used to make their way up and down the river guided only by one or two men with a huge oar—today, however, they are generally pulled by a tug in a string of six barges since this is usually quicker and more effective. All the vessels using the port make use of the tides, but not necessarily for motive power— mostly they are concerned with the depth of water in the river. The difference between high and low tide is as much as seventeen feet on average below London Bridge and this can of course make all the difference to the ability of the larger vessels to reach the upper parts of the river. We shall become more familiar with the tides insofar as they affect navigation in Part II, but in this

43

Chapter we are more concerned with the need to contain the tides by building embankments—the price to be paid for locating a city on the banks of a tidal river.

Today the River Thames flows between man-made embankments for much, indeed virtually the whole, of its course from Teddington to the sea. Whenever the land abutting the river is low-lying it has been reclaimed by great embankments, usually earthen walls outside the towns and London itself, and these rise sometimes to as much as twenty feet above the surrounding land. For as long as man has remembered, these embankments have existed. Who first built them? This question puzzled the Elizabethan historians, and it is not really surprising that in the absence of any positive evidence they credited the Romans with the achievement. After all, as William Dugdale in his great work *History of Embanking* (1652) pointed out, the discovery of Roman remains in the low-lying parts of Southwark, parts that would certainly be under water now if it were not for the embankments, was strong evidence for the existence of these works in Roman times. It was not until the late nineteenth century that this belief was challenged. Mr Spurrell, in an important article in the *Archaeological Journal* in 1885, first put forward the startling suggestion that the River Thames in Roman times was quite different from what it is today . . . that it was much shallower and indeed scarcely tidal at all above London Bridge. Thus riverside areas that would today be inundated by every high tide would then have been above all but the highest tides. This was the explanation for the Roman remains found below high tide level, and ever since then evidence has been accumulating that Mr Spurrell's thesis is in fact the correct one.

The Romans did not build the embankments, not because they could not, but because they had no need to! It was only with the later subsidence of land level that embankments became necessary. From about the time of Edward II (1307–1327) there are many recorded instances of repairs to embankments along the Thames. The embankments were not built all at one time, but piecemeal as and when necessary, or when land reclamation was particularly profitable, over a long period of time beginning possibly even before the Norman period.

Quite apart from the changes in land level, the building of the embankments themselves had an important effect upon the régime

of the river. Whereas the tides had at one time been allowed to
dissipate their force over a wide flood plain, now they were
confined to a narrow channel so that they surged further up-river
and scoured the bed of the river more deeply. This was fine so
far as the navigation interests on the river were concerned, but it
created major difficulties of flood control for the authorities of the
City of London. A contemporary record from the end of the
twelfth century, for instance, blames the action of the tides for
the collapse of the walls and towers that once fronted the riverside within the City. When the wind was blowing from a
particular quarter so as to cause a ponding-up of water in the
North Sea, and this coincided with high tide, there was what is
technically called a "surge" (e.g. such as occurred in the great
floods of 1953). On these occasions the water came rushing up
the estuary and there was much flooding along the riverside. The
City was reasonably secure because it lay well above the flood
level, but all along the lower parts west of the Fleet flooding was
a major hazard. One of the earliest recorded floods was in 1236
when the Palace of Westminster was flooded and men rowed
through the Great Hall in wherries. Only a few years later, in
1242, there was another disastrous flood when the river at Lambeth
overflowed for a distance of six miles and people were riding
through the Great Hall on horseback. In 1663 Pepys tells of a great
flood when all Whitehall was under water: "There was last night
the greatest tide that ever was remembered in England to have
been in this river." If one studies the main tidal surges in the
Thames Estuary over the last few centuries it is remarkable how
they seem to come at intervals of fifty to seventy-five years.

To some extent Old London Bridge acted as a barrage restrict-
ing the force of the incoming tide, and reducing water levels above
the bridge. But after the central arches had been widened in 1759,
and the water mills removed, it was less effective from this point
of view, and after it was rebuilt it ceased altogether to have any
significant barrage effect. It was estimated in 1820, after the widen-
ing of the central arches, that Old London Bridge had the effect
of reducing high water level above the bridge by about one foot.
This may seem little enough, but at high tide it can make all the
difference between danger and disaster. It was no mere coincidence
that after the removal of Old London Bridge it was decided to
build the great embankments that we know today. But before we

consider these we must take a look at the developments that had
been going on along the riverside.

During the sixteenth and seventeenth centuries many large
mansions were built along the river bank westwards of the City.
These were generally built very near the water and had magnificent flights of steps leading down to the water's edge, sometimes with imposing water-gates, like that of York House still to
be seen in the Embankment Gardens. There were also some lesser
houses with more modest riverside access, and here and there
lanes ran down to the water's edge at right angles to the river.
Because of the great demand for riverside sites for houses there
were very few riverside walks or paths open to the public. The
riverside was more or less a private reserve of the great and the
public had precious little opportunity of enjoying their river,
except from the south bank which was most inaccessible. H. V.
Morton in his book *In Search of London* quotes the first impressions
of a French traveller, Peter John Grosley, who visited London in
1765 and had great difficulty in getting a clear view of the Thames
. . . "unless I entered the houses and manufactories which stand
close to the river".

The first major proposal for a public riverside walk within
London was by Wren in 1666 just after the Great Fire. He proposed that a strip forty feet back from the river between the
Tower and Temple Stairs should be preserved from all houses
sheds or cranes to form . . . "a commodious key from Blackfriars
to the Tower". However, his scheme was too revolutionary for the
City, it was never enforced and in 1821 the attempt was finally
abandoned. Another century and a half was to pass before any
further serious attempt was made to improve this stretch of river
for the benefit of the public.

In the second half of the eighteenth century there took place a
series of unco-ordinated developments which fell far short of a
continuous riverside terrace, but which served a valuable purpose
in showing Londoners what might be done with their river. In
1767 the whole Thames frontage along the Temple Gardens was
embanked and a uniform frontage created. Then in 1772 came the
first riverside terrace of any significance available to the public—
the Royal Adelphi Terrace. This great achievement of the Adam
Brothers consisted of a broad public promenade raised high above
the river on a row of arches, and behind it the impressive façade

of Adam-style terrace houses. A contemporary engraving of the Adelphi refers to it as having been designed to "keep the access to the houses level with the Strand and distinct from the traffic of the wharves and warehouses". Today one or two of the original Adam houses remain, one of them used as the Headquarters of the Royal Society of Arts, but the terrace has disappeared, and the site, once one of London's most popular riverside walks, is now probably the least frequented part of London's riverside. The Embankment Gardens now occupy the old river bed below where the Adam terrace stood, and until the opening of the old York Watergate a few months ago there was no means of access from the Strand to the Embankment Gardens between Charing Cross and the Savoy. The Adelphi development was followed in 1776 by the building of Somerset House, with its fine promenade again raised high above the river on a series of arches, with a great watergate in the centre. This is still one of the sights of London, although the construction of the Victoria Embankment in front of the arches has robbed them of their original function and makes them look somewhat out of proportion. There is still a mooring ring in the wall of Somerset House, a rather forlorn reminder of the days when the Thames washed its walls.

These developments of the late eighteenth century paved the way, but the nineteenth century was the great period of embankment building in London. It was then that the present pattern of riverside roads, walks and gardens was laid down. In 1820 Mr Mylne, the engineer who had just completed a new embankment from St Paul's Wharf to Essex Stairs, recommended that it should be continued in front of the Temple and Adelphi Embankments, i.e. roughly in line with the present Victoria Embankment. However, no action was taken at the time, mainly because of the opposition of the coal wharfingers of the Hungerford and Temple embayment. In 1840 the construction of the Houses of Parliament began on a promontory of reclaimed land at Westminster which jutted out a hundred feet into the river, and in that same year a Metropolitan Commission recommended that an embankment should be built right along the north bank of the river from Vauxhall to Blackfriars, thus rounding off the awkward gap that was developing between the new Houses of Parliament and the Temple Embankment. This was a period of intense public discussion about the future of the river, but so far most of the proposals

for embankments had been discussed in terms of improved
navigation of the river by confining the tidal scour to a narrow
channel. This had become an important objective since the
removal of Old London Bridge as the water could now ebb more
quickly and the water level at low tide was lowered. A considerably larger area of mud was now exposed every low tide
than had been usual before the bridge was rebuilt. Improved
navigation, coupled with the prevention of floods, had hitherto
been the main driving force behind the schemes for embankments, but now an altogether new factor began to assume great
importance—the main drainage of London.

The surface streams of London had by the mid-eighteenth
century become little more than open sewers. Most of them, such
as the Fleet, had been covered in by the early nineteenth century,
and they acted as the main sewers carrying away the rainwater
that fell on London's streets. House sewage mostly went to cess-
pools. However, after the water closet became in widespread use
about 1830, the cesspools could not cope with the flow of water
and house sewage had to be taken directly to the Thames. This
happened just about at the time when the removal of Old
London Bridge had begun to expose mud flats at low tide. The
inevitable result was that the river rapidly became fouled with
sewage and at low water the stench was appalling. One of the
worst affected places was the magnificent new Parliament
building where matters got so bad that there was even talk of
moving up-river to Hampton Court. Barry's fine new riverside
terrace was of little use when the stench drove you indoors.

And now cholera arrived on the scene. In 1832, and again in
1848 and 1853, there were serious outbreaks that roused great
anxiety and led to the setting up of special commissions of
inquiry. Naturally the fouling of the Thames, and the inefficient
working of the main sewers (which ceased to operate effectively
during high water as there was inadequate fall), were suspected
as the main causes. In 1848 a new Metropolitan Commission of
Sewers was formed and its first major act, sensible as it may have
been for the long run, was in the short run a disaster. They
abolished cess-pools. Instead every house by law had to have at
least one water closet, and tens of thousands of cess-pits quickly
fell into disuse. Henceforth all the sewage had to go directly to
the Thames and of course this merely aggravated the situation.

The Millbank Tower

Something clearly had to be done—and that urgently. In 1855 a Metropolitan Board of Works was established with the express task of designing a master scheme for the main drainage of London, and Mr Joseph Bazalgette, later knighted for his services, was appointed chief engineer.

The Bazalgette scheme was a simple one, and it killed several birds with one stone. For the north bank he proposed that there should be three main east-west sewers to intercept the sewage flowing transversely towards the Thames, and take it away to new outfall works at Barking. The first, the highest of the three, would follow the line of Hackney Brook; the second, at an intermediate level, would follow the slope eastwards of Oxford Street; whilst the third, at the lowest level, would run alongside the Thames intercepting all the sewage that would otherwise have gone straight into the river. All three would meet at Abbey Mills, where a pumping station would be erected, from whence it would be taken in one huge sewer to the Barking Outfall. For the south bank the proposal followed similar lines. The main intercepting sewers would meet at a pumping station to be built at Deptford, and the sewage would go from there to the outfall at Crossness just beyond Woolwich. The obvious place for the low-level sewer on the north bank was of course within land reclaimed by a new embankment; so it was that the need for a new sewage system reinforced the arguments for new embankments and gave the necessary spur to their construction.

In 1863 an Act of Parliament was passed making provision for the building of new embankments on the River Thames, and work started immediately on the new Victoria Embankment between Westminster and the Temple. Huge quantities of granite were brought by sea from Cornwall, Dartmoor and Lundy Island, and from as far afield as Wexford in Ireland and Brittany in France. By 1870 the Victoria Embankment, incorporating the new sewer, and also the new District Underground railway that had been incorporated into the scheme, was opened to the public. The Albert Embankment was completed in 1869 and the Chelsea Embankment in 1874; notice that all these lie on the outside bends of the river where the erosion is greatest. Thus the great embayment of the river at Hungerford disappeared and in its place there was a fine riverside walk, the first on such a scale that Londoners had ever enjoyed, and a much needed new road

4

Collier shooting Westminster Bridge

taking some of the pressure off the Strand, until then the only
road linking Westminster directly with the City. Several attractive riverside gardens were laid out on the reclaimed land, and
today these add much to the lunch-time enjoyment of nearby
office workers. The embankment made possible a neat solution
to London's sewage problem; without it the only alternative
would have been to dig a trench 60 feet below the level of the
Strand and the cost would have been enormous. The sewage
scheme operated very successfully, and remains in its essentials the
same today. To round off this success story, the material used to
fill in behind the new embankment wall was dredged from the
river itself with considerable benefit to the navigation of the upper
river. The building of these great embankments was indeed a
great achievement, and it is fitting that a bust of the man who
more than any other man was responsible for them, Sir Joseph
Bazalgette, should stand in the embankment parapet by Charing
Cross Station, about in the middle of his greatest work, the Victoria
Embankment.

The new embankments solved many problems, but there was
one they did not solve—flooding. In fact by narrowing the river
channel they may well have caused the dangerous tidal surges to
rise higher than they would otherwise have done, so causing more
damage, and penetrating further up-river. Just as the Chelsea
Embankment was being finished there was a great flood that
inundated many parts of the riverside. Naturally some people
blamed the new embankment. Then in 1881 came another great
flood. Riverside embankments were raised after this, but yet
another great tide came in 1928 and large areas of Thameside
below London Bridge, and around Millbank and Hurlingham,
were flooded. Fortunately at the time of the disastrous 1953 flood
the flow over Teddington Weir was below normal for the time
of the year and the peak of the storm surge did not coincide with
the time of high tide so that relatively little damage was done
within London. If less favourable circumstances had prevailed
the damage and loss of life would have been very heavy. The more
the river channel is narrowed by embankments, the higher those
embankments have to be to protect against flooding.

The story of London's embankments did not end in 1874. In
1910, when the new County Hall was built on the south bank
opposite Westminster, the opportunity was taken to extend the

Albert Embankment eastwards in front of the new building. For
years it stopped dead in front of an ugly welter of industrial
development, but as part of the Festival of Britain it was extended
round in front of the new Festival Hall to Waterloo Bridge.
Within the last few years it has been taken a short distance beyond
the bridge and now ends abruptly—rather as the Houses of
Parliament site must have done before the Victoria Embankment
was built. Towards the end of 1967 the Greater London Council
announced that a new Thames sidewalk had been planned for the
south bank between Waterloo and Blackfriars. Sir Joseph
Bazalgette first suggested this over a century ago, but it had to be
abandoned because of the opposition of the wharf-owners. Now
at last it will be built. On the north bank the Victoria Embankment has been extended for a short distance during the last few
years to provide an underpass to Blackfriars Bridge, and this also
ends abruptly just by Puddle Dock. It can surely be only a matter
of time before this is continued along the river front to the
Tower; the Holden-Holford Plan for the City of London
included a bold scheme for a pedestrian terrace along this stretch
of waterfront, but like so many other imaginative schemes it
seems to have been pigeon-holed somewhere. The Blackfriars
Underpass is surely the forerunner of many similar schemes to
deal with London's traffic problems by utilizing the river itself.
The recently published report "Whitehall: A Plan for the
National and Government Centre" by Sir Leslie Martin contains
a far-sighted proposal for the provision of a major roadway
by-passing the Houses of Parliament, to link the Victoria Embankment with Millbank, either by building a new embankment
and embedding two 3-way highways in it, or by placing them in
submerged tunnels placed in dredged trenches as is proposed for
the new Woolwich Tunnel.

Perhaps it is not stretching the title of this chapter too much
to include here some reference to the locks, weirs and barrages
of the Thames. Teddington weir was built in 1811 and ever since
then Teddington has been the tidal limit for the Port of London
and, since 1909, the up-river limit of the Port of London Authority. Since the main abstraction of Thames water for London's
water supply is made above Teddington, one object of the weir
is to prevent salt water from passing beyond this point. It also
helps in flood prevention. But Teddington is not the limit of

navigation by any means. The largest lock on the River Thames is located at Teddington and it is capable of taking a tug and a string of barges. Strictly speaking the Thames is only half-tidal above Richmond weir; there is a half-tide lock at Richmond which provides transit for craft when the weir is down across the river.

There are some people who believe that what London most needs is another and altogether more massive barrage and lock system located further down-river. As early as 1858 a Mr Robinson proposed that a dam should be built at London Bridge to create a tideless basin in which docks could be built upstream. However in view of the sewage problem which was uppermost in everyone's minds at the time the scheme never had any chance of success. In 1904 a Mr Thomas W. Barber, a civil engineer founded the Thames Barrage Association which eventually came forward with a recommendation for a barrage across the Thames at Gravesend. Again however the time was not ripe. The Port of London Authority had only just been formed and no one was in the mood to take such *avant garde* schemes seriously when there were so many more urgent, if more mundane, tasks to be tackled. In 1935 a second Thames Barrage Association was formed and this time it looked as though the Port of London Authority might give the proposal serious consideration when the war intervened and it had to be dropped. This scheme was for a series of sluices across the river just above the Royal Group of Docks, with locks for smaller vessels at either end and a ship canal, 500 feet wide, near the south bank. After the 1953 flood there was renewed interest in the idea of a Thames barrage, but this time with particular emphasis on the flood-prevention aspects. The Greater London Council have declared themselves in favour of the principle of a movable flood barrier below London, but the whole question of a barrage or flood barrier is now with the Ministry of Housing and Local Government. There are many aspects to this issue and it is not easy to see where the net advantage lies. The main arguments in favour of a barrage are the freeing of shipping from dependence upon the tides, elimination of mud banks, no hull strains from vessels lying on the mud, less costs of upkeep, better recreational possibilities, and the new road crossing provided by the barrage itself. On the other hand there are counter arguments. The main disadvantage would be the possibility of delays as vessels waited to pass through the locks; with about a thousand vessels entering and leaving the port every week the possibility of congestion is a very real one. Then there is the problem of how to get rid of decaying matter and flotsam and jetsam thrown into the river if the tides are excluded. Another major problem is that up-river navigation by sizeable vessels depending upon the rise and fall of the tide would become impossible. One suspects that the building of a Thames Barrage, like the Thames Embankments, will only come about when there is a sense of public urgency, and this seems less and less likely to happen the more the 1953 Flood is relegated to history.

THE RIVER EXPLOITED

"London's least congested main street"

The Thames "above the bridges" may indeed play a relatively passive role in relation to the great city through which it passes, but it is nevertheless an important vein, if not exactly an artery, of commerce. The tonnage carried along the upper Thames would equal that of some of Britain's other large ports. Moreover it is with the coasters and colliers, tugs and tankers, lighters and launches, that pass under the bridges that Londoners are most familiar. So in this chapter we take a river-gazer's look at the traffic flowing along what John Masefield called "The great street paved with water", and we take up position at the finest of all vantage spots for our purpose—London Bridge.

We are fortunate. It is just an hour or two before high tide and the river is high and flowing strongly. Where else in the world can you stand in the heart of a great city and watch a 10,000-ton ship being loaded only a stone's throw away? With hundreds of other lunch-time river-gazers we lean on the parapet of London Bridge and watch the crane drivers on their tall cranes lifting boxes of oranges from a Spanish freighter just in from Bilbao depositing them with unerring accuracy at the "loop-holes" or entrance hatches of New Fresh Wharf. We are probably the only ones present who realize that the crane stands exactly where Old London Bridge once stood, or that a few old stones of London Bridge lie in a forgotten churchyard as near to the crane as we are.

We stroll across the bridge to take a closer look at the row of steamships ranged along Hay's Wharf, which occupies the whole of the south bank between London Bridge and Tower Bridge. Here is a Dutch ship with 2,000 tons of butter and cheese which is just being unloaded and will go into the huge cold stores with ten million cubic feet total capacity. Next to it is a Danish ship unloading bacon, and beyond that are several barges from which butter is being unloaded. We can tell that they are refrigerated barges because the decking is painted white. This will be Australian or New Zealand butter brought up by barge from the ship in the Royal Group of Docks, or Tilbury. Hay's Wharf has had a history stretching back over three hundred years. When I wrote to the proprietors to ask for some information about the company's activities they sent me an informative and beautifully illustrated book by Aytoun Ellis called *Three Hundred Years on London River*, which told the story of Hay's Wharf from its beginnings in 1651 to 1951. The colour paintings illustrating the book are by the author's artist son Mr Gordon Ellis, and the frontispiece of the clipper ship *Flying Spur* about to enter Hay's Wharf in 1862 with tea from Foochow is a beautiful and evocative piece of work—especially when one has read the story of this occasion as the author tells it in the book. The *Flying Spur* had raced home from China with its precious cargo of tea and was the first to enter the Channel where it was becalmed. A tug offered the captain a tow for £100, but he refused and offered £50 instead. Whereupon the tug skipper declared that he would go and tow the *Fiery Cross* which also lay becalmed further astern. So it was that the crew of the *Flying Spur* had the mortification, after a gruelling race half-way round the world, of seeing their defeated rival pass them to become the first home with tea worth £1 per ton premium. The picture shows the owners of the *Flying Spur* waiting on the quayside to greet the captain—no doubt it was a frigid reception! This and many other stories are told in this book in a way which brings vividly to life the history of this great maritime enterprise.

I can recall several significant "miles" in various parts of Britain, such as the "Floral Mile" of Suttons Seeds at Reading, and the "Mile of Concrete" of a pre-cast concrete firm near Leicester, but Hay's Wharf is the most significant mile of all. This company owns almost a mile of the most valuable commercial waterfront in the Port of London, stretching right from Cannon Street Railway Bridge to Tower Bridge and beyond. From small beginnings as pipe borers for London's primitive water-supply system, the early members of the Hay family (the name Hay's

Wharf has nothing to do with the hay wharf that used to exist on the site centuries ago) built up the business by an astute series of vertical and horizontal integrations with other firms so that it is today the largest company of public wharfingers on the Thames. One striking example of vertical integration was the absorption into the Group of the Humphery and Green Lightering Company, owners of the well-known "Maltese Cross" fleet of barges. The book describes this gradual process which culminated in the construction of a new head office for the company in the 1930s. It is this building which is perhaps better known to the lunch-time river-gazers of London Bridge than any other commercial building on lower Thameside. I liked the author's reference to the sculptured reliefs on the façade of this building: "seen from the north bank, or from the eastern parapet of London Bridge, these sculptured details look for all the world like Chinese characters or Egyptian hieroglyphics." I must confess that that is exactly what I have always thought they were; in fact however they represent Capital, Labour, Commerce and Distribution. How greatly this building contrasts with its work-a-day neighbours; I may be wrong but I cannot think of any other purely commercial building below London Bridge that makes any pretensions at aesthetic quality. Today Hay's Wharf has about ten berths along this stretch of water and they are able to receive about twenty vessels a week. Most of them bring in foodstuffs of various kinds which are stored in great warehouses, cold stores and wine cellars along Tooley Street. The name Tooley Street is an interesting reference back to St Olave, the same man who destroyed the bridge many centuries ago. The derivation is not so unlikely as it may seem at first sight because in Old English the long "o" had the same sound as our present "oo" (I am grateful to Mr Aytoun Ellis for pointing this out). To commemorate the connection there is a bas relief of Saint Olaf on the corner of the Hay's Wharf head-quarters building. The wine is stored in cellars built into the arches of the railway embankment which carries the lines high above the flat land on the south side of the river. With all this emphasis on food it seems right that the London Provision Exchange should be located in Tooley Street.

Fascinating as it still is, the Pool of London (or more accurately the Upper Pool, i.e. the stretch of water between Cherry Garden Pier and London Bridge) would have been even more colourful in years gone by. Gone are the curiously shaped Dutch schuyts that used to cluster round the wharves of Billingsgate Fish Market. There is a pretty story that the Dutch continued to supply the City with eels during the Great Plague and in recognition of this they were given free moorings in perpetuity at Billingsgate. They stopped coming just before the 1939-45 War when they were superseded by more modern means of transport. Today, indeed, almost no fish is brought into Billingsgate by water, most of it arriving by rail or lorry from the other fishing ports. However, the Billingsgate porters still lend a touch of novelty to the London scene with their curious flat-topped hats. As we saw earlier, Billingsgate used to be the main landing place in London for all cargoes; it was only in 1699, when an Act was passed making Billingsgate a free port for the sale of fish that it became important as a fish market. Gone too is the old sprit-sail barge, the Thames sailing barge or "sprittie". There were 3,000 of these in the tideway fifty years ago, but by the end of the last war there were only seventy left, and today there are only one or two still afloat; some of them having been carefully preserved by private individuals, or by public companies like Tate and Lyle Ltd., to take part in the annual Medway barge race, still held each year. The Thames barge was a remarkable craft. It was designed so that it could be handled by one man and a boy, yet it could carry up to 300 tons of cargo, bricks, grain, cement, timber or some such commodity. It had a flat bottom and drew so little water that people used to say that a Thames barge could "sail anywhere after a heavy dew". It's design had been gradually adapted from the earlier sailing barges, and did not reach its final form until the late nineteenth century. In their hey-day during the 1880s and 1890s the Thames barges were a very common sight round the coasts of Britain and Europe, and it is even on record that one sailed across to South America. For fifty years or so the Thames barge was almost a symbol of the River Thames—now alas they are no more.

But enough of this musing on the past. Coming towards us from the direction of Tower Bridge is a "flattie" or "flat-iron" as they are affectionately called, one of the fleet of forty-seven ships, known as "up-river" ships because they pass under the bridges, that supply fuel to the great power stations above London Bridge. Each ship carries 2,000-2,500 tons of coal, mostly from the North-east Coast. When business took me to Newcastle-on-Tyne

recently I made a trip to Blyth specially to see the huge timber
staithes projecting out into the river from which coal is chuted
into the waiting colliers. Whole trainloads of coal can be dropped
through the chutes into the colliers in a remarkably short time.
At one time Blyth exported huge quantities of coal abroad, but
today it is used mainly for the coastwise trade to London. The
colliers that bring the coal down from the North-east are the
largest vessels using the upper river, and although I have been
watching them now for over thirty years I still marvel that such
large ships can negotiate the bridges, seemingly with only a hair's-
breadth clearance, without hitting them. They are designed of
course especially for this purpose, with their low superstructure,
retractable funnels, and telescopic masts (features which account
for their nickname), but still the navigation of the bridges calls for
great skill and fine judgement. These vessels can only make the
journey using carefully pre-arranged schedules based on the tide
tables. The ship coming towards us now has a draught of about
eighteen feet and as she passes beneath us the depth of water at the
Wandsworth Gas Works (this is her destination and is as far as the
colliers go) is at this moment three feet less than she requires to
come alongside. However, the tide is rising, and will continue to
rise as the ship continues her way up-river so that by the time she
arrives at Wandsworth there will be just sufficient water to enable
her to unload. The skill of course lies in allowing enough head-
room under the bridges, whilst ensuring sufficient depth of
water to come alongside on arrival. The men who pilot these
ships above London Bridge are called Bridge Pilots or sometimes
"hufflers".

    The story of "sea-coal", so called to distinguish it from charcoal,
which was also called coal until the seventeenth century, is one of
the most fascinating of London's river. The coal trade dominated
the traffic on the river for many centuries and still coal accounts
for a larger tonnage than any other import into the Port of London.
The trade dates from the thirteenth century, and probably earlier;
it is interesting for instance that the builder of Old London Bridge
(1176–1209) was one Peter of Colechurch, a reference to the
ancient parish of St Mary Colechurch which disappeared after the
fire of 1666. At the beginning of the seventeenth century there
were two hundred colliers supplying London with coal. By the
end of the eighteenth century about three-quarters of a million

tons of coal was brought into London by sea every year, and coal accounted for three-fifths of the total tonnage of all coastwise shipping entering London. There were 1,200 sailing colliers engaged in the traffic in 1850, two-masted vessels called brigs, and the congestion in the river at this time was frightful. The reader will recall how it was the opposition of the coal wharfingers of the Hungerford embayment which delayed for many years the building of the Victoria Embankment. The ramifications of the coal trade at this period indeed affected the whole development of the Port of London. Within a few years, however, the sailing colliers had virtually disappeared from the scene, their place being taken by the new steamships. Railways carried an ever increasing tonnage of coal, but London was growing so fast that the quantity carried by water continued to grow even although the proportion of the total fell. In recent years oil has been substituted for coal to an increasing extent, and now natural gas may in time become an important competitor to both, but still the coal traffic is one of the most important of the port. About 13 million tons of coal a year, two-thirds of the coal consumed in London, arrives by way of the River Thames, over a quarter of it being used in power stations and a third in gas works. The Central Electricity Board owns fourteen "up-river" colliers specially designed to pass under the bridges, and eight "down-river" craft that supply the power stations below Tower Bridge.

The oil tankers that supply the power stations and other industrial works in the upper river are similar in appearance to the colliers. These vessels bring oil to large depots in West London from which it is distributed by road tanker over much of Southeast England. It is the use of the upper river by these specially designed craft that has hitherto been one of the biggest obstacles in the way of a Thames barrage. These ships can only make the upper reaches of the river by using the tide and if the barrage were built they would not be able to make the passage.

Close behind the "flattie" is a line of six lighters, or barges, being towed by a tug. The Thames lighter, so called because when it receives a ship's cargo that ship has been "lightened", has been dubbed "the taxi of the port", and it plays a fundamental role in the whole operation of the port. No other large port in the world makes so much use of lighters as London. There are over 5,000 "dumb" lighters (i.e. lighters that have no engines) in the Port of

London, including 2,732 open lighters, 1,547 hatched lighters, 318 tank lighters, 149 insulated lighters, and 340 canal-size barges: they have a total carrying capacity at any one time of well over a million tons. Of all the general cargo passing through the Port of London about half is discharged over the ship's side into lighters. The line of barges coming towards us now has six barges in all since this is the maximum permitted under the regulations. There is a man on each barge, but they are certainly not dressed as seamen. They are "lightermen" and they belong to the ancient Company of Watermen and Lightermen. Watermen are those who are concerned with the carriage of people on the river, and lightermen are concerned with the carriage of goods. There is a curious explanation for the fact that there is one man on each barge, although he appears to have very little to do. These barges are carrying crates, possibly furs and general cargo bound for the warehouses at Queenhithe, and the regulations state that each lighter carrying this kind of cargo (called "quay" goods, after the Legal Quays at which such cargoes were traditionally landed) must be attended by one man. Barges carrying what are called "rough" goods, such as domestic refuse or coal, are not subject to the same regulation.

As they pass under the bridge we get a better view of the tug. It is diesel driven; the steam tugs are mainly used today for handling large ships as they are more expensive to run. The tugs seem to become more modern looking and streamlined every year, and ever more removed from the fussy and grimy little steam tug of yesterday. The diesel tugs make no smoke, but on the other hand they are more noisy than their predecessors.

The London lighter has a shape that never changes; there is a "prow" at each end which is sloping at an angle of about 35 degrees—this is known as the "swim" and it helps to keep the lighter controllable when it is being towed by a tug since it allows the wash churned up by the tug's propeller to escape more readily. The keel plate is continued along the middle of the rear swim as a fixed rudder—if it were to project beyond the stern it would be more easily damaged. This fixed rudder keeps the lighter on a steady course; when a tug pays off a string of lighters, leaving them to make the wharfside under their own momentum, it is obviously important that they will maintain the same course. With the self-propelled barges this consideration does not arise

and they usually have projecting rudders to give more manœuvra-
bility. Lighters have flat bottoms so that they can sit on the mud
without damage, but even so the stresses and strains are great if
they lie on an uneven river bed, which is why they have to be
made of strong steel. Lighters are nearly always moved by tugs
these days so that the sight of one or two lightermen guiding
their lighter (the proper term was "driving" the lighter) with a
16-foot oar or sweep, which used to give me many fascinating
hours of river-gazing when I was a young man in the City, is now
a thing of the past. It was amazing how far these men could take a
barge on a single "drive". As we found in our little experiment,
they could cover as much as fifteen miles before the tide turned.

Coming towards us from Cannon Street Railway Bridge is
another line of barges, but these are carrying "rough" goods—
they are loaded with domestic refuse. The barges have closed
hatches to prevent the contents from blowing about so the
nature of the cargo is not immediately evident, but the fact that
there are no men on some of the barges is a clue. These may have
come from the Grosvenor Canal Basin, just beside Chelsea Bridge,
the last remnant of the old canal that used to run inland to Pimlico
Wharf, about where Victoria Station now stands. The City of
Westminster uses this basin as a convenient loading point where
the refuse is dropped into the barges and then towed down-river
to be dumped on the marshes in the estuary. Or they may have
come from the ultra modern public cleansing depot and wharf on
Upper Thames Street, beside Cannon Street Station, where there
is a covered dock for the loading of the barges. The whole scheme
was planned by the eminent architect Sir Hugh Casson. Or
indeed they may have come from a dozen or so up-river loading
points, for most riverside boroughs send their refuse away by
water and this is an important traffic on the tideway.

Here comes a small coaster heading boldly up-river, keeping
to the centre of the stream to get the maximum benefit of the
flood tide. Clearly it is not, unlike the majority of steamers
entering this part of the river, going to stop in the Upper Pool.
Perhaps it has a cargo of cement (now usually carried in bulk),
timber or grain. It may be making for one of the many riverside
wharves in the Vauxhall to Brentford area. Some of these are
merely depots from which materials are distributed inland, but
others are located at factories which import materials by water—

nearly all the industries located alongside the river do in fact use water transport to some extent. There are great paper warehouses at Southwark from which the Fleet Street printing presses are supplied, and many food warehouses and breweries. The old Lion brewery has now disappeared and the Festival Hall occupies the site, but the lion, built of coade stone, stands outside County Hall at the entrance to Westminster Bridge. Barclay Perkins have their brewery at Southwark and Courages theirs at Tower Bridge. There are also distilling and milling works, chemicals and paints at Battersea and Wandsworth. All these factories are continuously receiving some or all of their requirements by water, sometimes direct by coaster and sometimes from ocean-going ships by lighters, and they in turn send many of their products down-river to be exported to all parts of the world.

Chugging down-river against the tide is a self-propelled barge. Unlike the dumb barges this cannot qualify for free entry into the docks because it has an engine. It is therefore unlikely to be carrying a cargo to the docks, instead it will probably be heading for the Medway. In effect it is acting as a cargo-carrier specializing in short river trips. It would be completely uneconomic to use these boats as ordinary lighters because their engines would be unused nine-tenths of the time.

Among the small craft moving constantly up and down the river we may see one of the black-hulled police launches of the Thames Division of the Metropolitan Police. Originating in 1798 this claims to be the oldest organized police force in the world. It operates on the river between Teddington and Dartford Creek. There are twenty-two fibreglass police boats and nine wooden boats in service, together with three large twin-engined craft. The Headquarters of the Thames Division is at Wapping, but most Londoners are probably more familiar with the River Police station at Waterloo Bridge, the only floating police station in the world. Collectors of odd statistics may like to know that the Thames Police save the lives of about 150 people who fall or jump into the river every year—or at any rate they attempt to do so! We may also see a Port of London Authority launch on its regular patrol. The P.L.A. Assistant Harbourmaster, stationed at the Toll House, Kew, is in charge of the twenty-mile stretch between Teddington and Tower Bridge, and he maintains a daily patrol. His duties range from the supervision of the Oxford and

Cambridge Boat Race to the berthing of a 7,000-ton ship in the Upper Pool.

So we have passed an hour or two on London Bridge, and in that short space of time we have watched a great hive of activity, and the movement of cargoes totalling many thousands of tons. If all this had been loaded on to lorries it would have required many hundreds of vehicles since six lighters alone would carry nearly a thousand tons of cargo, equivalent to about seventy lorry-loads. Yet never is there any serious congestion on the river. No wonder the Thames has been called "London's least congested main street".

POSTSCRIPT

With this chapter of the book in mind I went one sunny morning in April to the new floating restaurant at Charing Cross Pier both to have lunch and to observe the traffic on the river at close quarters. This restaurant is a new addition to London's waterside and was installed recently by Thames Cruises Ltd. as part of their face-lift for Charing Cross Pier.

I had chosen well; the tide was rising and the river was busy with ships heading up-stream on the flood. By the time I had finished the soup I had counted half a dozen oil tankers, and many smaller vessels. Somewhat to the surprise of the other occupants of the restaurant I had succeeded in getting a picture of a large collier about to make Waterloo Bridge—this was between the soup and the main course. By the time I had finished the meal my total tally was as follows:

Colliers	2
Oil tankers	10
Passenger launches	20
Tugs hauling up to 6 barges each	6
Police launches	2
P.L.A. vessel clearing driftwood	1
Other small craft	5

I regard this list as the credit side of the account, for watching the passage of these ships added greatly to the enjoyment of the meal. But on the debit side I must put the prodigious quantities of flotsam and jetsam that floated past. I counted about twenty plastic washing-up liquid containers, before giving up in despair, not to mention a varied assortment of bottles and tins. But the plastic ones are the worst—they seem to be virtually indestructible and once in the river they float up and down with each tide, always more alien than any other articles one sees in the river. I also noted five heavy baulks of timber as large as railway sleepers, and of course a continuous assortment of smaller pieces of wood. What a pity it is that the tideway cannot be kept clear of this rubbish, it is unsightly and is a permanent hazard to all small craft on the river. I can vouch for the fact that it is no fun hitting a big piece of wreckage when you are in a rowing eight. On one such occasion the shell of the eight in which I was rowing crumpled under the impact and we found ourselves struggling in the water trying to get our feet out of the straps; a nearby police launch gallantly came to our rescue, but ran over the middle of the half-submerged boat and broke its back. Clearing the driftwood is one of the major tasks to be undertaken before a boat race takes place, and some of the rowing clubs located in the lower reaches are thinking of moving to the upper parts of the river in the hope of avoiding the worst of the driftwood. Even larger vessels are not immune. I well remember the excitement in 1955 when one of these floating battering rams pierced one of the pontoons supporting Westminster Pier and caused it to sink. The Port of London Authority collected nearly 7,000 tons of flotsam and jetsam in 1966 at a total cost of £60,000. It is odd that people who would never drop litter in the street will drop anything into the river without a moment's thought. Perhaps they forget that the tide which carries it downstream will bring it up again within a few hours.

It was as I was musing along these lines that I began to realize what the odd-shaped vessel I had noticed fussing about in the tideway was doing. It was one of the two special craft used by the P.L.A. to clear driftwood from the river. As it came nearer I could see its foreloader projecting over the bow, and on it were several large baulks of timber. It bore the name *Magog* and has a twin called *Gog*. As I watched, it broke off from its task and went to take in tow a small launch whose engine had broken down. By then I had finished my coffee and it was time to go. It had been a most interesting lunch.

Festival Hall terrace

6

THE RIVER ENJOYED

"And life ran gaily as the sparkling Thames"

A river gives to a city a very special character. Birmingham, for instance, seems to the Londoner to lack the kind of personality that the Tyne gives to Newcastle, the Humber to Hull, or the Thames to London. When we speak of Father Thames we have in mind a personality which is as inextricably linked to the personality of London as the voice is to the body.

Turner at the Pool, Chaucer at Southwark, Wordsworth and Canaletto at Westminster, Whistler at Battersea, Hogarth at Chiswick . . . they each saw the river in a new mood and gave it their own expression. Always the river is there, superbly the product of Nature in an almost totally unnatural environment. Still it glistens in the sunlight, boils in a storm, rises and falls with every tide, draws lovers to it in the moonlight, and murmurs ceaselessly of the lovely countryside through which it has passed and the deep ocean to which it must go. It is the townsman's umbilical cord to the World of Nature. Down the centuries he has felt an irresistible urge to enjoy his river.

From the earliest times there have been riverside walks and gardens, at first no doubt little more than footpaths along the river wall, but as the city grew so these riverside places became more frequented and were eventually laid out in a more formal way for the enjoyment of large numbers of people. These areas had perforce to be located outside the main built-up areas and were often situated on the more marshy ground which was not required for building. One can trace the movement of the "centre of gravity" of riverside recreation gradually westwards, as the city expanded. For a time there were pleasure gardens to the east of London Bridge, such as the Cherry Gardens of Bermondsey,

5

5

Victoria Embankment and Cleopatra's Needle

but the needs of the port took precedence and these disappeared, all except Greenwich Park which remains today almost the only substantial recreational open space in the Port of London. London's first main riverside recreational area was near Southwark along the south bank westwards of London Bridge. It was called Bankside, and dates from the early sixteenth century if not earlier. Here were the bear gardens, playhouses, taverns and brothels ("stews" as they were called), of London's most popular riverside resort. Bankside is of course renowned as the home of the Globe Theatre where Shakespeare's plays were performed, but it is interesting to recall that before the Globe was built there were round theatres at Shoreditch and Blackfriars just outside the City boundary. The City authorities refused to have them inside as they encouraged lawless assemblies of people and helped spread the plague. It was the attitude of the City fathers that led the theatre owners to look to the south bank where there had been a long tradition of performing plays in the courtyards of the many coaching inns in Southwark, a tradition which has been successfully revived at the "George" in recent years. So it was that the Globe came to be built on Bankside in 1598, of timbers brought across the river from the theatre at Shoreditch after it had been forced to close down. There is a plaque set into the wall of Barclay's Brewery marking the site. The Globe was only one of several round theatres built on Bankside at this time; others were the Swan and the Rose (built in 1592 and the scene of some of Shakespeare's earliest successes, both as an actor and a playwright). Many thousands of people paid their penny to cross the river to one of the many landing stages on Bankside in one of the boats which a contemporary visitor to London described as: "charmingly upholstered". Some of the Bankside theatres were used for bear- and bull-baiting (by British "bull" dogs), but others were used mainly for plays. It is astonishing that Shakespeare should have reached such a pinnacle of perfection as a playwright at a time when the theatre was only just coming into existence.

Southwark was also renowned for its great annual fair, one of the largest in Britain. Like most fairs it had begun as a market, but by Tudor times it had become primarily an occasion for general merry-making, with conjurers, jugglers, fire-eaters and dancers. It survived for several centuries until eventually it became too rowdy and had to be suppressed in 1763.

Southwark, being the bridgehead, was the first part of the south bank to become intensively developed, and this was one reason why the centre of gravity of riverside recreation moved away westwards. There had been a pleasure resort at Paris Garden near Lambeth Palace as early as 1600, and races, games and dances were held in the fields round about. The present Paris Street preserves the connection. In 1661 the Spring Gardens at Vauxhall (or Fawkes Hall as it was sometimes called) were opened to the public, and so began the famous Vauxhall Pleasure Gardens that were to play so large a part in London's social life for the next two centuries. The eighteenth century has been called the Golden Age of pleasure gardens, or places " . . . of polite amusement". The Vauxhall Gardens were laid out in formal avenues of trees and bushes, with less formal and more secluded walks for the younger people on the outside, and in the centre several elaborate and exotic buildings in which were held musical performances, balls and plays. Gargantuan dinners were served here.

Vauxhall Gardens came into existence nearly a century before Westminster Bridge was built, at a time when the only bridge across the river below Putney was London Bridge. This in itself is an indication of the extent to which river transport was used, and undoubtedly most people arrived by river. However, this may not always have been the most convenient means of transport, especially if one was dressed for a special occasion (the passage across the water is said to have played havoc with a well-brushed wig) and in 1742 the Ranelagh Gardens, just east of Chelsea Hospital and accessible without the need to cross the river were opened as a rival resort for the upper classes of society. The recreational centre of gravity had moved westwards again. The new venture was a great success. The central feature was a vast Rotunda, about 150 feet in diameter (as wide as the Reading Room at the British Museum), and this was used as a main concourse and for balls and musical performances. Many famous people and nobility frequented the Ranelagh Gardens and spoke glowingly of its merits. But in the sphere of recreation fashions are notoriously fickle, and by the turn of the century the Ranelagh Gardens had fallen out of favour. In 1803 they were closed down, and in 1826 the site was acquired by the adjacent Chelsea Hospital. Today visitors to the annual Flower Show are walking, all unknowingly, over the site of the great rotunda, the broad tree-lined avenues, the great fountain, the decorative canal and the Temple of Pan.

Another long stride westwards came in 1843 when the Cremorne Pleasure Gardens were opened at the western end of Cheyne Walk, Chelsea. Cremorne was never as fashionable as Ranelagh and was patronized by the lower middle and working classes. This may indeed have been its undoing for it eventually acquired a reputation for rowdyism and in 1877 it was closed down, the site being eventually used for the Lots Road Power Station in 1904.

On the south bank a parallel westward migration was taking place. In 1859 the Vauxhall Gardens closed down, and the site was quickly swallowed up in a sea of houses and factories. Today only two street names, Tyers Street, after the man who redesigned the gardens in 1728, and Spring Garden Lane, a mean little alley under the railway line, remain to remind one of two hundred colourful years of history. However, as one park closed another opened. In 1859 Battersea Park was opened. The site had been marshy and the levels had been built up with material excavated from the Royal Victoria Dock which was being built at this time. The process took several years but was brought to a successful conclusion thanks largely to the interest taken by Thomas Cubitt the builder who had created the new Pimlico. The new park, although much bigger than the Vauxhall Gardens, was by comparison a soulless affair, typical of the duller inner suburban parks of London. I remember as a boy in my teens walking eight miles through London streets to Battersea Park only to find there a small boating lake and some tennis courts. In 1951, however, all this was changed when it was decided to locate the 1951 Festival Gardens there. Now London has its Vauxhall Gardens back again and a glance at the old prints of those gardens suggests that even the buildings of the 1951 version are remarkably similar to those of two centuries ago. So the story of London's pleasure gardens is brought right up to date. Maybe the Battersea Festival Gardens are not exactly a match for the Tivoli Gardens in the heart of Copenhagen for instance (they were in fact modelled on the old Vauxhall Gardens), but they do bring a splash of colour and life into a rather drab corner of London's riverside, and on weekends and Bank Holidays the numbers using the Gardens frequently reach six figures.

The westerly movement of London's riverside recreational centre of gravity received a setback, a welcome setback, in 1956 with the opening of the new Mermaid Theatre at Puddle Dock. The City of London offered the site, occupied by a blitzed warehouse, to the Mermaid Theatre Company for the peppercorn rent of £100 per annum. At the opening ceremony in October 1956 the Lord Mayor of London, Sir Cuthbert Ackroyd, read the charter: "We, the Lord Mayor and Aldermen and Commonalty of the City of London, at the contemplation of the letters of Bernard Miles and other poor players of London, and having regard to the fact that Her Majesty sometimes takes delight in such pastimes, do welcome the said Bernard Miles and his Mermaid Theatre Company to use the exercise of playing at Puddle Dock. . . . " And so have the people of London, in the way that matters most of all to "poor players"—with their feet! No site could be more fitting, for right opposite, in Printing House Square, is the site of the old Blackfriars Theatre where some of Shakespeare's plays were presented. Indeed the site of the Mermaid Theatre was itself proposed for a theatre in 1616 but the City authorities feared that the actors might be tempted to steal from the royal wardrobe nearby and refused permission. The roof of the new theatre is a concrete barrel-vault type, one of the largest of its kind in Britain, but as the old warehouse walls on which it rests are four feet thick it has an assured base. This is more than a theatre, it is a club where people can meet and discuss the theatre or just enjoy a meal and a smoke overlooking the river; it was built by the people (the money was raised by public subscription) and belongs to them—it is not profit making—it has that indefinable something called "atmosphere".

The river is more than a passive back-cloth to London's pleasures, it is a source of pleasure in its own right. From very early times there have been river pageants of such magnificence that historians have recorded them in great detail. Pageants like that which took place when Queen Elizabeth, at the time of her coronation, took a ceremonial journey down the river from Westminster to the Tower with the Lord Mayor and City dignitaries: " . . . their barges decked with banners of their crafts and mysteries, artillery shooting off lustily as they went, with great and pleasant melody of instruments."[1] In the film *A Man for*

[1] Quoted from *London's Riverside: Past, Present and Future* by Eric de Mare, p. 75.

All Seasons there is a sequence showing Henry VIII being rowed down the Thames in the Royal Barge accompanied by his court. The barges were built to the exact specifications provided by the National Maritime Museum, but unfortunately for London's river-gazers the film was shot not on the Thames but on the Beaulieu River. In the seventeenth century the annual Lord Mayor's Show on the river (it was transferred from the land to the river in 1454 and reverted to the land in 1856) reached a peak of sumptuous extravagance, and in 1624 the Merchant Taylors alone spent over £1,000 on their display, a very large sum for those days. The Lord Mayor, in common with most men of high rank, had his own ornate state barge rowed by as many as twenty oarsmen, and a magnificent sight it must have been. Most of the great livery companies had their own state barges kept specially for use in the annual procession and for other state occasions as they arose. At Stationers' Hall in London can be seen a beautiful scale model of the Company's 1820 barge. For over 200 years the barge of the Stationer's Company had preceded the Lord Mayor's barge in the procession to Westminster. It was propelled by eighteen oarsmen, and there were several musicians on board. The barge was eventually bought by an Oxford college.[1] Many old prints of the seventeenth and eighteenth centuries, and especially the paintings by Canaletto of London rebuilt after the Great Fire, show these barges in the river; they lend a magnificence to the scene more usually associated with Mediterranean Venice than grey old London as we know it.

This period was indeed the hey-day of social life on the River Thames. Not only was there the ceaseless to and fro of people one would expect to see in the streets of any great city but there were occasional events of splendour and pomp that still excite the imagination. Whenever I hear Handel's Water Music I picture the lavishly gold-ornamented Royal Barge gliding down

[1] The barges were occasionally used for less formal occasions when the members of the Company, accompanied by their wives, would take a trip up the river to Richmond, serenaded by the musicians. The wine bill for one of these expeditions, preserved in the Company's archives, makes interesting reading:

12 bottles of Rhenish	£1 10
14 bottles of Port	£1 8
15 bottles of Lisbon	£1 10
There is also an item: Music	£5

the river with its attendant lesser vessels, and fireworks lighting up the sky as one of the popular "tableaux" is staged in front of the Palace of Westminster, with its dragons and other monsters belching out smoke and fire as the barges on which they are mounted are drawn in front of the excited crowds. On other occasions a new ambassador would be making his ceremonial journey up-river from Gravesend to the Tower escorted by the Lord Mayor and the City Companies, or King Charles II would be out in the river sailing his newly acquired yacht and founding, in effect, a new sport. Lesser folk also enjoyed the river in the more modest wherries which plied in their thousands up and down, and across, the river. In Tudor times Stow records that there were 2,000 wherries operating on the Thames, and by Pepys' day there were about 3,000 watermen working the river between Westminster and London Bridge alone, with as many as 40,000 between Windsor and Gravesend. This is indeed a staggering figure, and illustrates how completely river transport dominated the scene at this time. Samuel Pepys went "by water to Whitehall" as naturally as Sherlock Holmes went by cab to Baker Street. As late as 1822 there were still 9,000 watermen earning their living on the river, but already a new era had begun with the arrival of the steamboat.

The first steamboat was launched on the Thames in 1801, but it was not until 1815 that the steam packets, with their characteristic thin funnels and great paddle wheels became familiar sights on the river. Soon the "Penny Steamers" were carrying vast numbers of passengers, and new resorts came into vogue further downstream at places like Gravesend and the Rosherville Gardens nearby, Southend and Margate. The old Penny Steamers had a comparatively short hey-day, but in that period they carried millions of passengers on the river and gave great enjoyment to huge numbers of people. Before the days of the railways and motor-cars they were the first real means of mass transportation. By the latter half of the nineteenth century the faster trains had almost completely eclipsed the steamboats, although a few continued to operate such as the "Eagle" Steamers from Tower Quay. I have a vivid memory of sailing down the Thames to Margate on the *Royal Eagle*—as a child before the last war. I can still see the huge gleaming crankshaft heaving up and down as it turned the great paddle wheel—surely there could be no more thrilling

beginning to a holiday for a child. The last of the "Eagle" paddle
ships ceased to operate from Tower Pier some years ago, although
the last surviving paddle steamer on the Thames, the *Medway
Queen*, continued to operate from Rochester until late 1965. For
a while during 1967 the old paddle ship *Queen of the South* was
operating on the Thames, but this was no revival of the paddle
ship as such. The *Queen of the South* was frankly billed as a
veteran—the car has become an old crock![1] The larger screw
ships that used to operate from Tower Pier to Southend, Margate
and Ramsgate have had a thin time since the war, and in December 1966 the General Steam Navigation Company decided to
sell their three pleasure cruise ships, the *Royal Daffodil*, *Royal
Sovereign* and *Queen of the Channel*. The *Queen of the Channel* will
continue to sail the Channel under the flag of Townshend Ferries
running no-passport trips to France. The *Royal Sovereign* has also
been acquired by Townshends, but not for passenger service;
she will be used as a freight carrier on the Dover to Belgium run
where her speed of 21 knots, more than many cargo ships, will
be put to good use. During the Dunkirk evacuation the *Royal
Sovereign* rescued 8,000 British soldiers from the beaches; she
carried 157,000 passengers down the Thames as recently as 1961.
The *Royal Daffodil*, with its capacity of 2,385 passengers, more
than the *Queen Mary*'s, has been sold to a Belgian ship-breaking
firm. The sale of these three ships virtually brings to an end a
century and a half of pleasure cruising down the river. "It is sad",
commented a spokesman for the General Steam Navigation
Company, "but they are victims of the changing pattern of life;
whereas Mum and Dad used to take the children down the river
by ship, now they are taking them by car to the Continent."

With the eclipse of the Penny Steamers London seemed to turn
its back on its river. Few people travelled along it any more. This
became a matter of concern to many people, and there were
spasmodic attempts to revive passenger services on the river, one
of the most notable being the experimental waterbus service introduced in 1948 but it was not a success and was suspended in 1953.
With the great increase in tourist traffic in recent years there has
been a remarkable upsurge of activity on the part of small pleasure

[1] According to the Coastal Cruising Association there are only nine paddle
steamers still operating in Britain, and by 1970, unless urgent steps are taken to
preserve them, there could well be none.

craft running trips lasting only an hour or two. Because of the
high costs of operating river steamers, and the variable nature of
the British climate, the launch operators are having to confine
their activities to the short period during the summer when London is crowded with visitors—usually from mid-May onwards.

It is just possible that a new chapter in the story of the Thames
as a pleasure highway is just beginning. I refer to the hovercraft.
Already trials have been made on the tideway using the Denny
Hovercraft, and apart from the menace of driftwood these were
successful. The pilot said afterwards that he spent more time
looking for driftwood than actually driving the craft. It was the
danger of driftwood fouling the screw that caused the trials to be
discontinued; however, I am told that fresh trials are to be made
using a hovercraft designed to operate with an air-screw and this
should overcome the driftwood obstacle. One of the great assets
of the hovercraft is of course its speed. A race was held recently
between an Austin Princess and a hovercraft. They started from
Tower Pier at the same time and the object was to see which could
reach Southend Pier first. Despite the fact that the car made rapid
progress along the Southend Arterial Road it was still only thread-
ing its way through the outer suburbs of Southend when the
hovercraft arrived, skimming over the Southend mud fifteen
minutes ahead. Another argument in favour of the hovercraft is
that it makes little wash and the heavy wash sent out by conventional craft often causes considerable damage to smaller vessels
moored in the river. Because of its speed and other advantages a
hovercraft is to be included in the new London Fire Brigade
Station to be built near Cannon Street. As the era of the pleasure
steamer and paddle-ship draws to a close it is possible that a new
chapter is about to open with the hovercraft.

In the years ahead we are also likely to see a lot more of the
helicopter than in the past. The Battersea Heliport is inconveniently
sited British and European Airways hope to operate a new helicopter service between Heathrow, and Gatwick, and a new floating heliport to be located by the south bank opposite the Temple.
This is a very "dead" part of the river and has obviously been carefully chosen with the noise factor in mind. The ten months' experimental service in 1955/6 led to so many complaints about the
noise that it was withdrawn. That was with single-engined helicopters; now the much noisier twin-engined twenty-six-seater

Sikorskis are being proposed. Somehow helicopters always seem to rivet the attention more than traditional aircraft, no matter how familiar with them one becomes, and the noise is particularly difficult to ignore. Yet anyone who has fumed in the airport bus beleaguered in a traffic jam a mile from the Cromwell Road Air Terminal will appreciate the advantage of a fifteen-minute flight direct to the city centre. It looks as though we shall have to get used to the noise of helicopters as well as sonic booms.

Among the most colourful spectacles on the River Thames today are the two boat races, the annual Doggett's Coat and Badge race on August 1st organized by the Company of Watermen, and the Oxford and Cambridge Boat Race usually rowed in March or April. The Coat and Badge Race was instituted in 1716 by the Irish comedian and Drury Lane actor, Doggett, who wanted to encourage the London watermen. The race is rowed by six Thames watermen who have just completed their apprenticeship, and the prize is an orange-coloured coat and silver badge plus a small sum of money. It is the oldest sculling contest in the world. The Oxford and Cambridge Boat Race attracts a huge crowd every year, but as an oarsman myself I must admit to something of a chip on my shoulder. It always puzzles me that Londoners turn up in droves to watch two "foreign" crews, whilst only a mere handful turn up to watch their own London crews (and crews from all over Britain) row the Head of the River which is a far more impressive spectacle. There are as many as three hundred rowing eights taking part at one time and it is a wonderful sight. More than 3,000 competitors are involved at one time; this is a world record for the largest number of sportsmen engaged in a single event. The last time I participated we were crew number 267 and we had a long time to wait before it was our turn to hear the cox say 'Come forward'. This event takes place usually within a week or two of the Boat Race and is rowed in the reverse order, i.e. from Mortlake to Putney.

Pageantry has made something of a come-back on the Thames in recent years. In 1953 there was the magnificent river pageant to celebrate the Coronation of Queen Elizabeth II, and in 1965 the *Evening News* sponsored a fine pageant and firework display to celebrate the ter-centenary of the Great Fire of London; it was said that over a million people witnessed this impressive spectacle. But I remember most vividly of all standing on Westminster Bridge on V.E. Day watching the firework displays and hardly daring to believe that the war was over. On great historic occasions like this a kind of homing instinct draws the Londoner to his river just as it has done over the centuries.

One of the most ancient and colourful of Thames pageants is the annual swan-upping which takes place every July. There are about 600 swans on the River Thames and half of them belong to the Queen, the others being shared equally between the two London companies, the Vintners and the Dyers. Every year the young swans or "clearbills" have to be caught to have their bills notched. This is no easy task as the parent birds have first to be immobilized by tying their wings and legs together, before it is safe to handle the young. The bills are then notched, two notches or "nicks" for the Vintners and one for the Dyers, the birds belonging to the Crown are left untouched. The old inn sign "Swan with two necks" is a corruption from "Swan with two nicks". Every July several boat-loads of men colourfully dressed in blue and white, with the company pennants flying from the stern, set off from Blackfriars for four days of swan-upping. They are observing a tradition that spans the 700 years since Richard the Lion Heart is supposed to have accepted the gift of a swan whilst in Cyprus, so introducing that beautiful bird to our waters.

One source of recreation on the river which has given much enjoyment in the past, but which has diminished greatly in the last century, is angling. At one time the people living on London Bridge could trail lines in the river below and hope to catch a salmon, but that was before the river became polluted so badly. Because of the deterioration in the purity of the Thames waters extensive improvements were made in the 1950s to the sewage outfalls at Barking and Crossness, and there have been encouraging signs since then that fish are returning to the Thames. Even salmon have been taken from the filter screens of Fulham Power Station, and porpoises have been sighted as far up-river as Dagenham. Perhaps the Thames will again become popular with anglers, just as the fishermen of Stockholm fish the waters of the city with their picturesque nets. But the Thames will never become a clear flowing stream—its course lies over alluvial mud and it is there-fore always likely to be muddy; but there is all the difference between pollution and siltation. Long before the Romans landed on our shores the Britons had christened their river "Tamesis", or "dark river", and dark it will always be. But at least it need not be polluted.

No account of how Londoners enjoy themselves and their river would be complete without a mention of its riverside walks, parks and pubs. Walks like old Strand-on-the-Green wonderfully preserving its quiet village atmosphere; Maids of Honour Row at Richmond; Cheyne Walk at Chelsea, London's house-boat village; the Lower Mall at Hammersmith, long known as "Little Wapping"; miniature Bankside, memorable for its view of St Paul's across the river—the view that its builder Wren saw coming to life as he lived here during the building of the Cathedral; and the little riverside walk opposite the Greenwich Naval College whose name I have forgotten, but whose view I shall never forget. And parks like Richmond Park, the largest urban park in England, larger even than Newcastle's Town Moor, and with a genuine sense of remoteness and peace to which the deer contribute not a little; Kew Gardens so beloved of Londoners; Syon House seen from across the river, and indeed the whole of Syon Reach, the most beautiful below Teddington. And then the many riverside pubs with names that evoke whole chapters of history, the Doves at Hammersmith, the London Apprentice at Isleworth, the Prospect of Whitby at Wapping. The list is endless, London's riverside presents an ever-changing kaleidoscope of Life in all its forms, in all its moods. One can only repeat Dr Johnson's famous aphorism: "He who is tired of London is tired of Life."

7

THE RIVER ENNOBLED

"London, flower of cities all"

If it is true that the river lends a nobility to the buildings upon its banks, then it is equally true that the buildings, or the best of them at least, ennoble the river. Throughout the centuries public buildings have been located on the banks of the Thames to take advantage of the fine setting that such a location affords. Buildings like Somerset House, County Hall, the Festival Hall and many others contribute as much to the enhancement of the river as they themselves derive from it.

But the earliest buildings located on the riverside were usually sited with other considerations than beauty in mind. Defence was often the primary consideration. Take the Tower of London for instance. There it stands, a great square Norman keep built by an alien king to subdue his conquered people. By a curious irony of history it has become almost a symbol of London itself, rather as Caernarvon Castle has become to the Welsh—that too was built by an alien English king to subdue his rebellious subjects. It may be, as tradition has it, that there was a Roman fort on this site performing the same guardian role, but there is no real evidence of this. The Tower was built by William the Conqueror in 1078 and the site was carefully chosen because it lay on the perimeter of the City, yet beyond its control being a royal palace, and on the water's edge so that supplies could be brought in by water: Windsor Castle was built at the same time as a support. The square Norman keep was built of white freestone from Caen which was painted white after it had become discoloured through weathering; it came to be known as the White Tower and was for centuries a landmark to seamen navigating the lower reaches of the river. The Tower at one time acquired a somewhat sinister reputation, having been a prison, armoury, citadel, place of public execution, and the Royal Mint. But it has lived down its past and is now regarded with affection by Londoners. I fancy, however, that most Londoners are content to see it there, solid and slightly mysterious—they watch the thousands of visitors waiting to go inside, but do not themselves have any desire to enter—they prefer to keep alive the aura of mystery, intrigue and murder that still clings to the solid pile. Theirs is the Tower of the Traitors Gate and the Black Ravens—the Beefeaters and the Crown Jewels are for the tourists.

Only one other building on Thameside today can be said to owe its existence to considerations of defence, and that, strangely enough, is the Parliament Building. When people were discussing what to do after the great fire of 1834 had destroyed the old Palace of Westminster, there were suggestions that it should be removed to Green Park or to the present site of Buckingham Palace, but the old Duke of Wellington pointed out that the Houses of Parliament should never be situated in a position where they could easily be surrounded by a mob. It will be remembered that this was the time of the Chartist riots, whilst the French Revolution was still within living memory. This argument won the day and it was decided that the new Houses of Parliament should be built on the site of the old. A competition was held for a design in the Elizabethan or Gothic style, and was won by Charles Barry. Building started in 1837 and was completed, apart from the towers, by 1857. In the next three years the Victoria Tower (336 feet high) and the Clock Tower (329 feet) were added. Big Ben, now the universal symbol of London, first began to boom in 1859. The name is derived from Sir Benjamin Hall who was Commissioner of Works at the time, and of course it really refers to the bell and not the clock. So well made was this great clock that never has it erred by more than four seconds from Greenwich time, and it has only failed twice, one of those occasions being in 1944 as the result of an air raid. Above the clock a light shines when the House of Commons is sitting, a tradition begun in 1893. I am told that there is a restaurant opposite the House where a red light shines when a division is being taken in the House, and that many an M.P. has had to make the agonizing choice between his rump steak and party loyalty. The Houses of Parliament are medievalism gone mad, yet they are magnificent—there is no other word. I confess to an intense dislike of anything Gothic, but somehow the Houses of Parliament never seem to come under that umbrella, although according to the celebrated architectural historian, Dr Pevsner, they are: "The most imaginatively planned and the most excellently executed major secular building of the Gothic Revival anywhere in the world."

The alternative title of the Houses of Parliament, the Palace of Westminster, reminds us that the building occupies the site of the medieval palace of the kings of England. The Great Hall of Westminster, first built by William Rufus in 1097, and reconstructed with the great hammer-beam roof we know and admire today in 1398 by Richard II, is the only part of the Old Palace still remaining. The fact that probably few people looking at the Houses of Parliament from Parliament Square realize that the Great Hall in the foreground is 500 years older than the rest of the buildings around it, is itself a tribute to the way in which Charles Barry integrated the medieval structure into his Victorian complex. The custom of bowing to the Speaker's Chair in the House of Commons is a reminder that in the days before 1834 the House of Commons used to meet in the Chapel of St Stephen in Westminster Palace, when it was customary to bow to the altar of the chapel. Indeed the very design of the debating chamber today obviously owes a lot to its origins in a chapel. It will be recalled that Edward the Confessor located his Palace at Westminster primarily to be near his new Abbey, and I am tempted to include Westminster Abbey in this review of riverside buildings. But this would be rather stretching the point.

Convenience for industry or commerce has of course been the primary reason why many buildings have been located by the riverside, but seldom can such buildings be said to ennoble the river, usually very much the reverse. No one can say, for instance, that the jumble of industrial and commercial buildings along Lower Thames Street, Bankside, or Nine Elms, add any beauty to the river. Apart from the fine Georgian warehouses in the West India Dock, there are only two buildings associated with trade and commerce that come to mind as lending dignity to the Thameside scene. Both date from the early nineteenth century, although earlier buildings occupied each site for centuries before that. They are the Customs House, located between the Tower and London Bridge, and Fishmongers Hall, alongside the latter. The Customs House might be called dull by some, yet it has an impressive dignity of its own, and it possesses a short tree-lined quayside fronting the Thames which could add greatly to Londoners' enjoyment of the river if only they were allowed to use it! One wing of the Customs House was bombed during the war and bears the inscription: "This wing destroyed in 1940, rebuilt to maintain the historic succession of customs houses on or near this site, was opened by Her Majesty Queen Elizabeth, 8th June 1966." Geoffrey Chaucer belongs to that "historic succession". Between 1374-86 he was Comptroller of the King's Customs in the Port of London. This is the fifth Customs House on this site; all the previous buildings were destroyed by fire. Fishmongers Hall, by London Bridge, is a well-proportioned structure in the Greek Revival style built in 1831. In Fishmongers Hall is preserved the actual dagger with which Sir William Walworth, Lord Mayor of London and a member of the Company, slew Wat Tyler in 1381 and so brought to an end the Peasants' Revolt.

In the days before even horse carriages were widely used, ready access to the river was almost an essential requisite for all the larger buildings—especially those used by the members of the public. Today only a few of these buildings survive, but perhaps the most important are the two great ecclesiastical buildings on the south bank, Southwark Cathedral and Lambeth Palace. Only a small part of the present Southwark Cathedral, part of the square tower, dates from the fourteenth century, but in the south chancel can be seen the tesselated pavement of a Roman villa that once stood on the site. For most of its long life the cathedral (which only became a cathedral in 1905) enjoyed a fine situation at the south end of London Bridge, but during the nineteenth century the riverside became heavily industrialized and the cathedral became sandwiched between ugly warehouses and factories on one hand and a railway viaduct on the other. No other church of its size and consequence in London has suffered so ignominious a fate, and although the present Bishop of Southwark has made a virtue of necessity by emphasizing that the church exists to serve the work-a-day world around it I think most people would feel that the sooner the cathedral is restored to its rightful setting by the riverside the better; happily there are some

Embankment art show

moves in this direction now. Lambeth Palace has been used by the
Archbishops of Canterbury as their London residence for seven
centuries; it is conveniently close to Westminster whilst being on
the Canterbury side of the river. The great gatehouse, with its
two impressive towers, dates from 1490, and it stands virtually
unchanged today. Part of the palace now serves as a hostel for
visiting Anglican bishops from the provinces and overseas.

The Tudor and Stuart periods saw the flowering of the great
riverside palaces of London, particularly between Westminster
and Blackfriars on the north bank. Apart from the fine banqueting
hall by Inigo Jones in Whitehall, which dates from 1622, only
one or two small fragments from these buildings have survived to
the present day. These include the Watergate of York House in
the Embankment Gardens, recently restored and now in use once
more as a gateway, and the steps leading down to where the river
once flowed past the old Whitehall Palace, now the new Air
Ministry building in Whitehall Gardens. When the foundations
for this building were being dug they came across the fine wine
cellar of the old Palace built by Henry VIII. It lay in the path of
the foundations for the new building, but rather than destroy it
they moved the whole structure bodily a few yards and incorporated it into the basement of the building. I have attended
several orchestral concerts there and a more historic setting for
Handel's music could hardly be imagined. Although the old
buildings themselves have disappeared, the names still remain.
Names like Whitehall itself, named after Henry VIII's great
palace, York House and Durham House on the other side of
Charing Cross Station, and the Savoy further east still. The chapel
of the old Savoy palace has survived and after having been
extensively modernized is now used by the Royal Victorian
Order; the name of the old palace is continued in the Savoy
Hotel and the Strand Palace Hotel. Each of these great palaces
had its own elaborate riverside terraces and stairs, and if Canaletto
painted a fair representation of what he saw, the Thames at this
period must have presented a more noble spectacle than at any
other time before or since. This was not only because the buildings presented their most noble aspect towards the river, but
because the river itself was an animated highway uniting the
whole.

With the nineteenth century and its new patterns of transport

6

Ancient Queenhithe
Cannon Street Station

and its rampant industrialism, standards of taste declined, the era of gracious living was gone, the Thames became merely an economic asset to be exploited by warehouses or factories, or an awkward barrier to be spanned by iron railway bridges. However, even during this period there were isolated buildings that enhanced the river, buildings like Hawkshaw and Barry's Cannon Street Station with its massive walls and its huge twin towers symbolizing the abounding confidence and pride in technical achievement so characteristic of the Victorians. The station has just been rebuilt but the towers are still standing; it would be a pity indeed if they were to disappear from the river scene. On a lesser scale, but very familiar to those who have gazed idly out of the window of the train as the driver waits for the green light to enter Victoria Station, is the Western Pumping Station of the London County Council (now the Greater London Council). Built in 1875, this is a rather pleasing example of how a style usually associated with an altogether different function, in this case the French châteaux style, can be applied successfully to an industrial building. It stands in marked contrast to the huge Battersea Power Station on the opposite side of the river which was designed by Sir Giles Gilbert Scott in 1933. He has since designed another like it, the Bankside Power Station, which aroused so much opposition just after the war because it obscured the view from St Paul's Cathedral. The Bankside Power Station excited little attention from the architectural point of view, but the Battersea Power Station was hailed as setting a new pattern for industrial architecture as a genre in its own right and not merely using styles borrowed from other fields.

We come now to the last and most controversial group of buildings that ennoble London's river—those that have been erected there primarily to take advantage of the riverside setting. In this group must be included most of the major public and private buildings erected on the riverside in the past few years. Foremost among these is the Festival Hall, built as part of the Festival of Britain in 1951, but only now being finally completed. Few public buildings have had more influence on architectural style than this one, and the Festival of which it was a part. To those of us who remember the austerity of the war-time years, and the sense of disillusion of the immediate post-war period, the Festival of Britain stands out as a symbol of the beginning of a new and brighter world. There was a light-hearted gaiety about the buildings that suddenly lifted us all out of our war-weariness and lethargy. New shapes and new materials caught us by surprise; even the litter bins were attractive. However, not all the subsequent buildings on Thameside have sustained this high promise. For example the new buildings fronting the Albert Embankment, a solid rampart of buildings each as undistinguished and indistinguishable, as the next, have none of the lightness of touch of the Festival Hall, or of that very successful building on the opposite bank—the Millbank Tower. This is a building which truly uplifts the soul as well as the eye (it is the tallest building in London). It soars skyward, a slender glass-sheathed tower perfectly related to its base podium. I have some business acquaintances who are fortunate enough to have rooms on the upper floors and I can vouch for the fact that they have as fine a view of the River Thames as can be had anywhere in London. Unfortunately the members of the public are not allowed on to the roof of the building. The heavy monolithic pile of the new Shell building near County Hall is not so successful. It is altogether out of keeping with the idiom of the times. It is a curious reversion to the style of architecture that produced its pre-war cousin the Shell Mex building on the opposite side of the river, best known perhaps for its massive clock nicknamed "Big Benzine" (it is in fact larger than Big Ben) and very useful for a time check when coming into Charing Cross Station. But at least the top floor of the Shell building is open to the public, and the view from here, twenty-seven storeys high, is truly magnificent. This, together with the new Post Office Tower, meets a long-felt need in London for high viewing platforms. When I was on the Shell building recently the attendant was watching me like a hawk and when I got into conversation with him he told me that only an hour or so previously a young man had hurtled 351 feet to his death from the open-sided balcony on the river side. The newest building of all in this group is the Queen Elizabeth Hall, alongside the Festival Hall, and the most enigmatic of them all. To me it is the ugliest new building in London, a fort of a place, brooding and forbidding, dark and uninviting, massive as a Maginot pill-box ... everything in fact that a concert hall should not be. I grieve for such a lost opportunity on a peach of a site—the Thames deserves better than this.

There are also a few older buildings that qualify for inclusion in this group. The County Hall, for instance, was obviously designed to make the maximum use of its very fine situation across the river from Westminster. It is in the "Beaux Arts" style and has a heavily colonnaded frontage which looks grim close to, but certainly presents a fine aspect seen from across the water. Dating from the turn of the century is the Tate Gallery, a nicely proportioned building in the Greek style which was presented to the nation by the sugar magnate Sir Harry Tate. In the last year or so it has been the practice for the Queen to greet her distinguished guests at the Tate Gallery rather than at Victoria Station, a very happy innovation as there could be no finer backcloth than the Thames. A little further up-river is Chelsea Hospital a very satisfying addition to the riverside scene. It was begun in 1682 to house retired and invalided soldiers, about 500 of them, and today they still wear the colourful uniforms of that time. The building is one of Wren's finest works, restrained and dignified. The name Chelsea, however, calls to mind not so much any particular building as a host of people, people like Carlyle, Whistler, Leigh Hunt, Brunel, Rossetti, Turner, Mrs Gaskell; these and other Chelsea inhabitants have ennobled the river more than its buildings. Chelsea is still the place to go and see people—not buildings. St Thomas's Hospital, on the southern bank, has none of Chelsea's restraint. Built in accordance with the ideas of Miss Florence Nightingale which she had acquired following her experiences in the Crimea, it is little more than a row of large rectangular boxes placed end-on towards the river and joined together by a long inter-connecting spine. The main object was to keep the patients in one part of the hospital isolated from those in another since Miss Nightingale had discovered during the Crimean War that disease spread so rapidly in hospitals that it was safer to keep out of them if possible and let Nature effect her own cure. The hospital was badly bombed during the last war and is now being extensively reconstructed.

It is not only buildings that ennoble the river; we must include also the monuments. Cleopatra's Needle, for instance, lends interest and a focal point to Bazalgette's Victoria Embankment which would be too uniform without it. The whole beauty of Cleopatra's Needle is that it has no practical purpose whatever; it just looks right where it is. Whether it would have fitted as well in Parliament Square, its first intended destination, is more doubtful. The Needle has had a curious history. As the inscription says, it lay "prostrate for centuries on the sands of Alexandria", until it was towed to England in a cylindrical iron barge built especially for the purpose. The journey was an eventful one for the cylinder had to be cast loose during a storm and had to be recovered later by another steamer and brought back to Ferrol in Spain before the journey could be resumed. It was eventually erected on its present site in 1878. The Monument in the City performed a similar role to Cleopatra's Needle—it acted as a focal point at the north end of Old London Bridge as may be seen from early engravings of London in the eighteenth century. Now of course it has lost this role, yet it is still in Defoe's words "a beautiful column". The Monument was not strictly speaking erected as a memorial to the Great Fire, which destroyed 13,000 houses but killed only four people, so much as to the speedy rebuilding of London. When one recalls that Sir Christopher Wren came forward with his plan for rebuilding the City only four days after the last embers were extinguished, one has some idea of the sense of urgency which activated people at the time. In a way this was a pity because it meant that people were so anxious to rebuild quickly that they rejected any large-scale alterations to the City as it had been—thus only a small part of Wren's far-sighted proposals was in fact carried out. Some people have declared that the coincidence of the Great Fire starting in Pudding Lane and ending in Pie Corner is proof of Divine condemnation of the excesses of a gluttonous age. But this theory falls down somewhat when one realizes that Pudding Lane was so called after the "puddings" or entrails of animals which were conveyed by this route from the butchers' establishments in the City to the dung boats on the Thames!

The statue of Queen Boadicea at the northern end of Westminster Bridge occupies a very significant point at the beginning of the Victoria Embankment and near the spot where the Romans are thought to have first crossed the Thames. It is a vigorous piece of work and worthy of its fine setting—at least I think so. I know that Dr Webster the archaeologist has other views; he has contemptuously dismissed it as having: "the appearance of an armoured milkfloat". A monument of a different kind, but beloved of those who know their London, is the group "The

Burghers of Calais" which occupies a surprisingly modest, if on reflection very apt, position in the shadow of the Victoria Tower.

Last but not least come the ships whose sailing days are over. Scott's *Discovery*, built with wooden sides two feet thick to resist the Antarctic ice, was once a scout headquarters, but is now an escort ship to H.M.S. *President* and H.M.S. *Chrysanthemum*, training ships of the London Division of the Royal Naval Volunteer Reserve. The Admiralty have adhered to their undertaking, on assuming control of the *Discovery*, to allow the public access to the ship on every afternoon. H.M.S. *Wellington* is the only floating hall of a City Company, namely the Honourable Company of Master Mariners. Like the Needle, these ships play a valuable role in adding visual interest to the long sweep of the Embankment. When H.M.S. *Chrysanthemum* was taken away for a refit in 1965 Kings Reach seemed dead without her.

So we end our short excursion round some of London's riverside buildings, not on the land but on the water. For however much Man may try to ennoble the river, his work lasts for only a short span and then decays and eventually disappears. There is a brewery where the Globe Theatre stood, and a rubbish shoot where vessels once lay at anchor in Dowgate Harbour. The river alone remains unchanged and unconcerned. The river is the thread upon which we mortals hang our beads from time to time.

PART TWO

THE PORT OF LONDON

8

INTRODUCING THE PORT

In Part One we were able to speak of the river as a familiar friend, one whom every Londoner already knows, and every visitor quickly discovers for himself. We could assume at least a casual acquaintance if not an intimate knowledge. But now we have to introduce the river of the port—an unknown river even to the vast majority of Londoners, and certainly to almost every visitor. Probably not one in a thousand readers has secured the necessary pass to penetrate behind the high walls of the great docks, although more may have taken one or other of the various cruises down-river, particularly those organized by the Port of London Authority which actually enter the Royal Group of Docks. This indeed is the only way effectively to see the port and in the following chapters we shall take a trip down the river to Gravesend. But first we take a look at the port as a whole and consider how it came to be the third largest port in the world, handling 59 million tons of cargo per annum and 250,000 passengers, and accounting for nearly a third of the value of all trade in the United Kingdom.

For all but the last hundred years of its existence the Port of London has been used mainly by sailing vessels, since steam propulsion did not come into widespread use until the middle of the nineteenth century. It is therefore important to consider the geography of the port in relation to its use by sailing ships. The considerable tidal rise and fall was a great asset to sailing vessels because it meant that even if the wind was against them they could utilize the power of the tide to move up-river where it was difficult or impossible to tack, and of course the rising tide gave adequate depth of water in nearly all stretches for at least part of the day. By carefully judging the tidal rise and fall, and making the maximum use of the wind, a vessel drawing up to eighteen feet could make the whole journey from Gravesend to the Pool on one tide. With an unfavourable wind it would only be able to reach one or other of the patches of deep water or "pools" or sometimes "holes" around Erith or Woolwich. The pilot's main anxiety would be that a fog might descend whilst he was passing from one such pool to another and he would be forced to press on in spite of the danger for fear of running the ship aground on the shallow reaches. Even with the wind in a favourable quarter sailing vessels could not easily negotiate the several "U" turns in the river without the tide to help them. The advent of steam diminished to a great extent the dependence of vessels on the tide for motive power, but the changeover was associated with an increase in the size of ships and so the importance of the tide in ensuring an adequate depth of water under the keel was magnified. Vessels bound for the Royal Docks, for instance, will wait at Gravesend until low water, or an hour or two after, and then proceed up-river with the rising tide so that they arrive off the

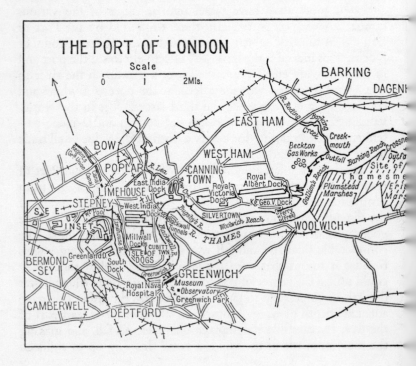

dock entrance just before high water. So far as small non-powered craft are concerned the tide still plays the role of an auxiliary motor; with the tide running at between two and five knots an hour a vessel can expect to be carried nine to fifteen miles by tidal currents. The tide is the most important feature of the geography of London River so far as the shipping on the river is concerned; without it the port could not survive.

The history of the Port of London can be summed up in a word—migration. It is the story of the gradual migration of ships and docks and harbour installations downstream, either in search of adequate depth to accommodate vessels of ever-increasing draught, or because there was insufficient space in the crowded upper reaches for the building of docks and wharves. Until the sixteenth century the Port of London was co-terminous with the City. It was represented, as we have seen, by the harbours of Queenshithe and Billingsgate, and the various wharves between them. But then came the great expansion of trade in the Eliza-

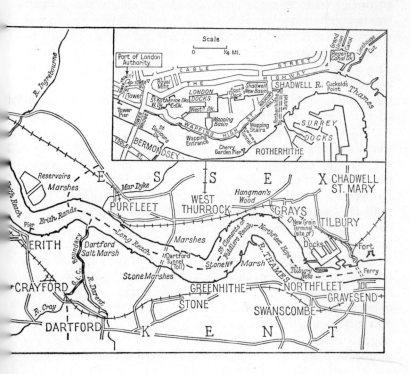

bethan era and with it a substantial growth in the size of ships. Warships in particular grew rapidly in size to accommodate the largest possible number of guns, and these were in the van of the migration downstream which began at this time.

Queen Elizabeth, and those who succeeded her on the throne, actively supported by the City Fathers, did their best to prevent this migration downstream, by imposing severe limitations on the landing of goods at wharves other than those licensed by the sovereign. The Exchequer derived a substantial part of its revenue from customs duties on imports, whilst the City were anxious to keep control of the trade passing through the port. The problem of collecting duties on imports was a difficult one. It was solved by nominating certain parts of the riverside as "Legal Quays". Goods subject to import duties could be landed there and nowhere else. These quays were situated on the short stretch of river between London Bridge and the Tower, and the resultant congestion was appalling. The City was reluctant to do anything to encourage trade to move downstream, but clearly the position was fast becoming impossible, and so from time to time additional wharves were licensed to receive dutiable imports; these came to be called "Sufferance Wharves" and they were situated below the Tower as far as Hermitage Steps, and along the south bank between London Bridge and St Saviour's Dock. This remained the position until 1800, with the Port of London confined in effect to the short stretch of river one mile below London Bridge . . . but it was bursting at the seams, and it was obvious to all that something would have to be done.

So far the migration downstream which began in Elizabethan times had been of a rather special character. In 1513 the Royal Dockyard had been established at Deptford, and it remained there until 1869 when it had become obsolete owing to the increasing size of vessels. The dockyard built many quite large ships, including the first ship built for the East India Company, the *Trades Increase*, 1,200 tons, built in 1607, and the largest ship of her day. Henry VII established another dockyard at Woolwich and the famous *Henry Grace à Dieu* was built there. As trade with overseas territories expanded so the size of vessels increased. The East Indiamen were the largest vessels in service and they were too large to use the upper reaches of the river so they discharged their cargoes at Blackwall where a wet dock was built as early as 1660

for the fitting out and masting of vessels. The masting shed
rose six storeys high and towered above the flat undeveloped
marshland; it was for many years a landmark for miles around.
Because of the congestion in the upper reaches there was obviously
no room for fitting-out basins there, so these tended to be established farther downstream. They were not insignificant in size.
With its two basins, the Brunswick Dock at Blackwall could
accommodate up to sixty ships. In 1696 the Howland Wet Dock
was built on the Surrey bank, where the present Greenland Dock
is situated. This was no more than an enclosed sheet of water
where vessels could be fitted out away from the crowded river—
it had no warehouses and did not operate as a modern enclosed
dock as no goods were landed there. None of these developments
directly challenged the trading monopoly of the Legal Quays
and the Sufferance Wharves, but they demonstrated that wet
docks were possible and gave a natural focus to the agitation that
was now building up for a complete overhaul of the port.

Unless one has seen a contemporary engraving of the port
around 1800, showing as many as ten tall-masted ships lying side
by side in the Pool, a fantastic mêlée of masts and rigging, it is
difficult to imagine how congested it had become. It is recorded
that 1,775 vessels were allowed to moor in the Upper Pool where
there was only space for 545, and in addition there were about
3,500 barges and other small craft trying to move about or merely
moored as floating storage depots. Ships frequently had to wait
as much as a week for a vacant berth, and it is said that the river
was so crowded that even a small boat could not get across. The
quays became so congested with goods, especially the Legal
Quays where there were added delays because of the shortage of
Revenue Officers, that vessels often had to wait to unload even
when they were moored alongside. Utterly inefficient though all
this was yet it must have presented a magnificent sight. It stirred
a contemporary poet to describe the scene in these words:

> Hail Prince of Rivers, Great Augusta's[1] pride,
> Source of that wealth to other ports deny'd
> As swells thy breast, magnificently gay,
> A thousand barks their silver sails display

[1] The Romans officially renamed Londinium "Augusta" in recognition of
its wealth and importance, but the name never stuck.

Fraught with the treasures of the distant poles
Or where Marmora laves or Ganges rolls
For they all proud, they furl the canvas wing
Still breathing odours like a fruitful spring.
Pacific Thames—the while thy turrets rise
And fame thy story tells to distant skies
May no rude foe from foreign shores conveyed
Disturb thy waters or confound thy trade.

Perhaps the most important single cause of congestion was the huge fleet of sailing vessels bringing coal to London. Around 1800 three out of every five coastwise ships entering London were colliers. In an article in the Port of London Authority *Journal* Mrs G. W. Howe has quoted a contemporary description of "coal dust hanging like a permanent cloud over the Lower Pool, with as many as ninety coal brigs discharging cargoes into up to a dozen barges alongside each of them". Because of its low value relative to its weight, coal is an expensive commodity to transport by road so all the brigs wanted to come as far up-river as possible, and being dependent upon the winds they tended to wait for suitable wind and tide conditions in the lower river and then came crowding into the upper reaches all at the same time. London's port was being throttled by coal, and at the same time its people were being suffocated by smoke from a million coal fires. Yet within two decades coal had supplied its own solution—steam to drive the new steam-ships and the new turbines to generate electricity.

Other evils followed in the train of the general congestion. Fires were frequent and very costly, and in severe winters ice forming in the river above the bridge would break away and come crashing down among the crowded ships causing considerable damage. But it was the losses from systematic and organized thieving and plundering that caused most alarm of all. There was a veritable hierarchy of crime. Most audacious of all were the "River Pirates", well armed men who would cut a boat adrift from its moorings, follow it downstream until it went aground and then swiftly remove its contents before daybreak. Then there were the "Light Horsemen", often Revenue Officers or the mates of ships, who would steal from the ships at night, and "Heavy Horsemen" who had specially large pockets built into their clothes into which they could slip tea or sugar stolen from the ship; or "Lumpers" who would throw stolen objects overboard so that their accomplices the "Mudlarks" could recover them from the mud at low tide. The City authorities were nominally responsible for the maintenance of law and order in the river, but they could not stop the plundering. Dr Patrick Colquhuon in his influential book published at this time, *Commerce and Police of the River Thames*, stated that 10,850 out of a total of 36,344 persons working in the port were known to be thieves or the receivers of stolen property. It was obvious that unless something was done the trade of the port would suffer, and opinion crystallized round the view that enclosed wet docks were the best solution. In 1799 the West India Dock Act was passed authorizing the building of a new dock in the Isle of Dogs. A year later a stone was set into the river wall at Wapping fixing Trinity High Water as a datum for the construction of docks on the River Thames. It was the foundation stone for one of the greatest achievements of any nation at any time—the building of the largest system of wet docks in the world.

The City authorities struggled to the last to prevent the expansion of the port downstream. They recommended the cutting of a new canal right across the middle of the Isle of Dogs to enable vessels to by-pass the awkward "U" in the river; whilst one commentator of the period went further and suggested the straightening of the river itself by creating a new channel across the Isle of Dogs and Blackwall Point, the original river bed to be used for docks. However, by now it was commonly agreed that wet docks were the proper solution and the City opposition was in vain. In the event both the new West India Dock and the City's canal across the Isle of Dogs were built, the dock in 1802 and the canal in 1805. The canal was an immediate failure. Vessels had to be towed through it by rowboats, or by gangs of men as depicted in a contemporary engraving by William Daniell, and the whole operation took almost as long as going round by river. But the new dock, complete with its own Legal Quays, was an immediate success. It inaugurated a dock mania that lasted for most of the century.

The Port of London Authority have in their possession a wonderful collection of engravings by William Daniell of the building of the new docks, and I am most grateful to the librarian for allowing me to inspect them. They give a vivid impression

of the massive scale of the works undertaken at this time, and the
captions convey the sense of pride which the people of the time
must have felt. Typical is this caption to the "View of the New
Dock in Wapping" dated 1803:

> This great public work is conceived on a scale calculated to support
> the dignity of the nation and the important interest of its commerce,
> and will when completed, in conjunction with other magnificent
> works either in preparation or contemplation, render this Metropolis
> ultimately the First Port, as it is already the First City, in the World.

The details of how the various docks were built must await
our trip down the river, but for this outline of the port's history
suffice it to say that during the nineteenth century five great dock
systems came into being, the India and Millwall Docks (1802–
1868), the London and St Katharine Docks (1805–58), the Surrey
Commercial Docks (1807–64), the Royal Docks (1855–1921),
and the Tilbury Docks (1886). By the end of the century London
was equipped with a larger area of enclosed water than any other
port in the world.

The five main groups of docks that comprise the Port of
London were all built by private enterprise—after the railways
possibly the greatest achievement of private enterprise in the
nineteenth century. But as with the railways the competition
between the different dock companies became so fierce that
eventually it threatened to ruin all of them. The London and
St Katharine Dock Company stole a march on their competitors
when they acquired the Victoria Dock in 1864 (it had been built
by the Victoria Dock Company), but in 1886 their rivals the East
and West India Dock Company retaliated by building the new
docks at Tilbury. Rate cutting and the duplication of dock
facilities reduced profits so drastically that by the end of the
nineteenth century it had become apparent that complete integration was the only effective solution for the smooth operation of
the port as a whole.

Another problem facing those anxious to improve the facilities
of the port at this time was that of dredging. With the rapidly
growing size of vessels during the latter half of the nineteenth
century it was becoming obvious that the present arrangements
for dredging were quite inadequate. Before 1857 the Trinity
House had enjoyed the privilege of taking sand and ballast from

Tower Bridge

the river, but they operated only ten miles from London Bridge, and they were really interested only in lifting saleable ballast—they ignored the shoals of mud which were increasingly impeding access to the upper river. The Corporation of the City of London had for the last 600 years been responsible for the conservancy of the river from the estuary up to Staines. However, in recent years they had not pursued their task with the vigour necessary to meet the changing circumstances. Public criticism led eventually to the transfer of the conservancy powers from the City to the newly created Thames Conservancy in 1857. As if to symbolize this event the Lord Mayor's Show transferred from the river to the shore in that year and has remained land-based ever since. However, the new Thames Conservancy still tended to put the commercial value of the ballast above the requirements of the port and their dredging programme was criticized as inadequate to provide the depth of water required for modern vessels. In 1905 an Act was passed stipulating that a depth of 30 feet at Gravesend shallowing to 18 feet at London Bridge should be aimed at, but by this time the conviction had become widespread that the control of dredging policy should be integrated more fully with the running of the port.

In 1908 these various pressures for an improvement in the administration of the port led to the passing of the Port of London Act which provided for the establishment of the Port of London Authority to administer the whole port from Teddington to the Nore. Since October 1967 the Port of London Authority has comprised not less than fifteen members and not more than sixteen. Interests represented include major shipping lines, trade unions, Trinity House and the Greater London Council. The Authority runs its own police force and Flying Squad (although the Thames Division of the Metropolitan Police is responsible for the river itself—the P.L.A. police cover the docks); it is responsible for the dredging of the river, removing almost two million tons of spoil per annum; it operates grain silos and other port installations; and it is responsible for the smooth running of the docks and the port as a whole. It is not however responsible for health matters which are in the hands of the Port Health Authority under the Corporation of the City of London, or for pilotage which is the responsibility of the Corporation of Trinity House. All in all the Port of London Authority (P.L.A.) has a tremendous responsibility, not

7

The Tower of London

least of its duties being the planning of new investment totalling
about £10 million per annum.

The reader may have gained the impression that the Port of
London is composed only of the five dock systems referred to
earlier; if so this is a false impression and must be corrected at
once. Professor Bird has estimated that during the decade 1947–56
only about a third of the ships entering the port berth in one or
other of the five dock systems (or about half the total tonnage as
a higher proportion of the large vessels use the docks) whilst only
about one-seventh of the tonnage of imports and exports passes
over the quays of the docks. The remaining ships are handled by
one or other of the many riverside wharves that line the Thames
from its mouth to Teddington Lock, whilst the cargoes that do
not pass over the quays at the docks are transhipped into lighters
over the ship's side and moved from the docks to wharves
elsewhere on the river. London has a huge warehouse capacity, it
is in fact the greatest warehousing port in the world. Behind these
statistics there lies a fascinating story that has already been touched
upon but not yet fully told—the story of the London lighter.

Because of the system of Legal Quays and Sufferance Wharves
adopted before 1800 the practice grew up of transferring goods
from vessels moored at these quays into lighters so that they could
be moved to other wharves and warehouses elsewhere in the river.
This practice had its origins, it will be recalled, back in Elizabethan times when certain goods had to be landed at Queenhithe
by order of the sovereign; because of the impediment of London
Bridge these goods had to be unloaded at Billingsgate and then
shipped by barge to Queenhithe. The use of lighters has the great
advantage that when a vessel arrives with several different types
of cargo these can be more economically distributed to their
respective destinations by water than they can by road—whether
the cargo is first deposited in a quayside warehouse and then
shifted by road or lighter, or unloaded directly into the lighter
over the ship's side. When plans were being made for the building
of the enclosed docks in 1800 the lighterage interests of the port
were fearful that their trade might be killed. However, they
managed to have a clause inserted in the West India Dock Act
1799 which virtually ensured their survival. This guaranteed that
lighters would be able to enter the docks to receive or discharge
cargo without paying any dock dues (subject to certain con-

ditions)—the celebrated "Free Water" clause. Events proved that the building of the docks have not in any way diminished the importance of the London lighter. Nor can this be ascribed only to the Free Water clause. The lighter is a basic necessity for the efficient operation of the port. According to Professor Bird there are over 600 wharves on the tidal Thames, and the lighters are the lorries which ply up and down this great commercial artery. As Professor Bird has put it: "The Thames is not only a 'highway' of approach for sea-going vessels steaming to their destinations but also a 'street' used by the internal tug-towed traffic of the port."[1]

The story of the port "outside the docks" is only partly the story of the London lighter. The other important feature which made the growth of riverside wharves possible was the granting of bonding facilities by H.M. Customs to certain warehouses. When dutiable goods enter the country the duty has to be paid at some place and at some time. The place is usually the point of entry, but what is the appropriate time? Often goods are imported to be stored for lengthy periods, perhaps until there is a demand for them or until they can be re-exported. It would be intolerable for the merchant if he had to carry the duty on these goods long before he could dispose of them. The device of the bonded warehouse was introduced to get over this difficulty. The goods are placed in the warehouse, which has two locks, one belonging to the Crown and the other to the merchant. The duty is only payable when in fact the goods are taken out of the warehouse to be sold in this country. Many of the early bonded warehouses were located in the new enclosed docks, but in time the Commissioners of Customs have created bonded warehouses at wharves up and down the river so that today there are about 170 firms with bonded warehouses.

The Port of London suffered very badly from German air raids in the last war, and much of it was damaged by fire and bombing. Because of its exposed position the Port of London was used only by essential shipping during the rest of the war years, and many of the ship repair yards and docks were used for warships or for the construction of the Mulberry Harbour components for the invasion of Normandy, or for the pipe line linking England with France: PLUTO.

[1] *Geography of the Port of London*, Hutchinson University Library, 1957, p. 117.

To end on a less sombre note, I would like to recommend readers to visit the headquarters of the Port of London Authority in Trinity Square, just by the Tower of London, to have a look at the magnificent model of the whole of the Port of London which is on permanent display in the vestibule. If this is inconvenient there is an exact replica in the Science Museum in Exhibition Road, South Kensington. May I also take this opportunity of recommending all those readers interested in the day to day developments in the Port of London to read that excellent house journal the *Port of London Authority Monthly*; it is packed full of interesting information about the river. But above all, if you are at all interested in the port, be sure to take one of the trips organized by the P.L.A. during the summer every Wednesday, Thursday (for children) and Saturday—you will sail right through the Royal Docks (provided shipping requirements allow) and it is an experience to remember. This is the trip which we shall make in the next chapter.

9

THE POOL OF LONDON
AND THE ISLE OF DOGS

We begin our river tour at Tower Pier and within minutes we are passing under the bascules of Tower Bridge into the lower half of the Upper Pool.

On the north side are the huge austere warehouses Hardwicke built for Telford's St Katharine Docks in 1828. There is a somewhat derelict air about these docks and indeed they are no longer used by shipping and are up for sale, probably as a housing site for the Greater London Council. It is perhaps fitting that this should be their destiny, for over 1,000 houses had to be demolished when the docks were built, including the ancient hospital and collegiate church of St Katharine, which left only its name behind. It was in fact the difficulty of clearing the site which explains why these docks are twenty-five years younger than the West India Docks, although they lie ten miles nearer central London.

Next to the moribund St Katharine Docks lie the London Docks which are very much alive. They are older than the St Katharine Docks, having been built (Western Dock) in 1805. As soon as the West India Dock had proved a commercial success after 1802, there were schemes for further new docks nearer the City to gain the benefits of proximity to the warehouses and markets of central London. At first the entrance to the London Docks was from the Upper Pool, but with the completion of the Eastern Dock (1815), and eventually the Shadwell New Basin in 1858, it became possible to enter from the Lower Pool and to build a larger lock entrance. The two older entrances are now closed and only the Shadwell Entrance is used. It faces eastwards and can easily be missed from a vessel travelling downstream. Because of their location so near the centre of the city these docks have specialized in the high-value, low-bulk goods like tea, coffee, spirits, drugs, ivory and canned goods. London Docks have twenty acres of vaults where casks of wine and spirits are kept in bond. However, modern techniques are rapidly changing the wine trade; the latest development is the erection of glass-lined ferro-concrete tanks on the quayside capable of holding half a million gallons of wine, the wine being pumped from bulk carrier vessels into the tanks and in due course into specially equipped bulk road vehicles. Wine tankers first began to arrive in the port in 1960 and now they are the normal method of bringing wine into this country. In the old days gangs of twenty-two men to each hatch were necessary to unload the wine casks, today the same quantity of wine can be discharged by nine men far more quickly. It is no longer safe to assume that the tankers you see on the tideway are carrying petroleum—they may be carrying Dubonnet! Wool is also an important commodity handled at the London Docks and there are nineteen acres of storage space for wool. The tops of the warehouses are generally set aside for show floors as they have the best light.

The area we are now passing on the north shore is Wapping and it has had a colourful history. There is not a lot that could be described as picturesque on our route so we must make the best of the "Prospect of Whitby" and the "Town of Ramsgate". The former, with its black and white exterior, stands out in marked contrast to the drab industrial setting; it dates back 300 years, although it was rebuilt in 1953–4, and the name recalls the sea-coal trade with the north-east coast. The "Town of Ramsgate" just by Wapping Old Stairs, most famous of all the stairs leading down to the river, is where the Ramsgate fishermen repaired to when they were bringing their catch up to Billingsgate. The name Wapping recalls criminals and police. The criminals were the pirates, like Captain Kidd, whose bodies were left for three tides to flow over them at Execution Dock, after which they were taken down to Bugsby's Reach and hung up as a warning to others; and the police have their river headquarters near Tunnel Pier, their launches can usually be seen in the river at this point. Wapping is only a shadow of what it once was. There are today only five pubs along Wapping High Street and Wapping Wall. But seventy years ago there were no less than thirty-six, and this district, together with Ratcliff Highway, was one of the liveliest and most notorious in all Dockland.

On the south bank lies Bermondsey, an ancient borough famous for its Benedictine Abbey and its tanning trade. St Saviour's Dock, a short inlet just opposite the Wapping Entrance to the London Docks, is all that remains of the old River Neckinger; it once figured in a Royal Charter conferring on the tanners of Bermondsey the right to use the tidal waters of the Thames for their requirements. Cherry Garden Pier, below St Saviour's Dock, is where the Upper Pool merges into the Lower Pool. The name reminds us of the times, long ago, when cherry gardens existed here, and Pepys went: " . . . by water down to Greenwich, and up to the top of the hill and there played cards. And so to the Cherry Garden and then by water singing finely to the Bridge", and when Evelyn also a great diarist lived at Sayes Court in adjacent Rotherhithe enjoying the rural seclusion of this quiet riverside spot.

At this point in the river we are passing over Brunel's Thames Tunnel. As this was built as near as four feet to the bed of the river in places vessels are forbidden to anchor over it for fear of causing damage. As we draw level with the Shadwell Entrance to the London Docks we are passing over the Rotherhithe Tunnel built by the London County Council and opened in 1908. The tunnel would have been built at the same time as Tower Bridge and Blackwall Tunnel if the L.C.C. had accepted the recommendations of a Select Committee Report of 1885, but they were not convinced that it was really necessary. However, as soon as it was completed it attracted 2,600 vehicles a day which fully justified the expense. On either side of the river can be seen the circular air vents, very attractive in their way—like rose pergolas without the roses.

Rotherhithe adjoins Bermondsey on the southern shore. It is another ancient borough which has played a major part in the maritime history of the capital. It was here that the great fleet for the invasion of France was fitted out by Edward the Black Prince; here Henry Reve built the first gunpowder factory in 1554; here the *Mayflower*, one of the ships of the local whaling fleet, ended its days in a shipbreaker's yard; here, in another Rotherhithe yard, the famous *Fighting Temeraire* was broken up after Turner, sitting on Cherry Garden Pier, had immortalized it on canvas. This transition from shipbuilding and fitting-out, to shipbreaking, is characteristic of several of these towns on the southern bank,

of Deptford and Woolwich as well as Rotherhithe. They all
began as shipbuilding yards and then, as the size of vessels
increased, turned to shipbreaking instead.

The river now begins its great "S" bend round the curiously
named Cuckolds Point in Limehouse Reach and then round the
great meander of the Isle of Dogs . . . sharp changes of direction
that were a real headache in days of sail. The term "reach" in
fact is related to the distance that a vessel could "reach" on one
tack before having to change to another. It comes as a shock,
when moving downstream along Limehouse Reach, to see Tower
Bridge away across the southern bank . . . the same sort of shock
that I used to get when standing on Westminster Bridge and
seeing St Paul's Cathedral in what seemed to be completely the
wrong position—one forgets to allow for the sharp bend of Kings
Reach. I often have fun asking my friends whether it is quicker
to go from Westminster to St Paul's via the north bank of the
river or the south. On the north shore we are now passing
Limehouse, once so famous for its "Chinatown" but today you
have to look hard to find it. The parish church of St Dunstan,
Stepney, has a special connection with the sea since every baby
who is baptized at sea has to be registered at St Dunstan's Church,
although the Rector tells me that this is now a very rare occurrence. Here the Regents Canal terminates at the Regents Canal
Dock owned by the British Transport Commission, and capable
of taking small coasters and short sea vessels. Goods can be transhipped into barges and taken from here by water to the Midlands
via the Grand Union Canal. Just below the dock entrance is the
Limehouse Cut, an artificial canal giving an alternative route from
the River Lea to the River Thames by-passing the Isle of Dogs. In
late Victorian times all the passengers would be busy staring at
what was then one of the curiosities of London—Fletcher's Yard,
now occupied by the British Dredging (London) Company.
William Fletcher found it difficult to excavate the marsh subsoil
for the graving dock he planned to build and in the end he
hit upon an ingenious solution. He acquired an old East Indiaman,
the *Canton*, and pinned her into the ground, removing all her
interior fittings, and replacing her stern with gates. This worked
excellently as a dry dock until 1898 when it was replaced by a more
modern dry dock.

The promontory of flat land that terminates at Cuckolds Point is now almost wholly given over to docks—the Surrey Commercial Docks. This, the only one of the five dock systems that is on the south bank, is one of the most intricate and confusing of them all. There are no less than eleven separate docks and they cover a water area of 159 acres. The water levels in these various docks are different and the reason for this is that, unlike the other docks in the port, these grew piecemeal without any overall plan. The Surrey Commercial Docks owe their origin to the Howland Wet Dock built in 1696. For its time, this was a great undertaking. It covered about ten acres of water to a depth of seventeen feet. Some 120 vessels could be accommodated at a time. However, it was not a commercial dock as it was not licensed to receive dutiable goods, it had no warehouses and cargoes were not landed there. It served as a fitting-out basin, and the proprietors hoped also to attract some of the overflow repair work from the adjacent Royal Dockyard at Deptford. The Howland Great Wet Dock was simply a sheet of water surrounded by trees to act as a windbreak; contemporary pictures show a complete absence of buildings round the dock except for a large private residence at the Western end belonging to the landowner on whose land it was built. It became very popular after the great storm of 1703 which damaged many ships in the open river, but whether this can really be ascribed to the trees is doubtful as they could only have made very small growth since they were planted only a few years before. In 1763 it became known as the Greenland Dock when it became the base for whalers operating in the Arctic seas, the first buildings being erected at about that time to handle the blubber and other by-products. They say that if you know where to look for it you can find the skull of a whale embedded in the wall of one of the sheds at the Greenland Dock.

In 1801 the Grand Surrey Canal Company was formed to build a canal from the Thames via Camberwell and Croydon to Epsom, and ultimately, it was hoped, to provide a waterway through to Portsmouth. In the event the canal never reached beyond Camberwell, but it triggered off a series of dock developments which far eclipsed in importance its original objectives. Various new docks were built around the canal and the Greenland Dock, which by now had come to be used exlusively for the import of Baltic timber and corn, and in 1855 a new company was formed to control the whole enterprise called the Grand

Surrey Docks and Canal Company. Today these eleven separate docks can berth a total of fifty-three ships, of which thirty-six are timber berths. The docks are associated particularly with the timber trade because in the early days they could not handle dutiable cargoes, and timber was the only commodity that could be landed without sufferance. Many of the docks are used for storing floating timber, especially the Stave, Lavender and Lady Docks which are relatively shallow. Smaller ships and barges at one time used the Surrey entrance, opposite the Shadwell entrance to the London Docks, but this has now been abandoned and all ships using the docks enter from Limehouse Reach into Greenland Dock. The timber trade is highly seasonal and during the height of the season some 500 barges may be in the Surrey docks, entering or leaving at the rate of about 100 a day. During the last war the enemy air raids caused terrible destruction in these docks, particularly from incendiaries. I still vividly remember seeing the glow in the sky when the Surrey Docks burned during the terrible weekend September 7th–8th 1940.

We now begin the long loop round the Isle of Dogs. How the island got this odd name is not known for sure. The most likely explanation is that it dates from the time when the Royal Kennels were established here in connection with the hunting activities at Greenwich Park. Another possibility is that it is a corruption of Isle of Ducks. In early times there was nothing here but flat uninhabited marsh, with only a pilgrim pathway leading down to the river crossing, and a chapel where the pilgrims, probably *en route* from Canterbury to Waltham, could rest and pray. Later several windmills were established on the island; they were built on the walls because their purpose was to lift the water from the drainage ditches on the island to the river—hence the name Millwall (and Millbank near Westminster). During this period the island remained uninhabited, not an island of dogs, but an island of sheep and possibly some cattle ready for the slaughterhouses of London. When the agitation for wet docks grew, around 1800, the Isle of Dogs was an obvious site. Not only was it unoccupied, in sharp contrast to the densely inhabited areas nearer the City, but it had access to the river on three sides, and the alluvial mud could easily be excavated, exposing a layer of gravel, about twenty feet below the surface, which greatly assisted the actual construction. The success of the West India Dock encouraged further development on the Isle of Dogs. In 1806 the East India Dock was built, in 1829 the moribund canal built by the City Corporation was sold to the West India Dock Company and after being used for a while for floating timber, was later widened to become the South Dock, and in 1868 the Millwall Docks were built, so completing the dock system on the island. The Millwall Docks were planned on a new principle. The idea was that the wharf-side sites would be let to major industrial undertakings for the construction of factories immediately adjacent to the dock. But in practice this did not work out as planned and the dock developed along conventional lines, grain becoming the principal commodity handled. Although there are only five docks in the India-Millwall group, compared with the Surrey Commercial's eleven, they are much larger and deeper and cover about the same total area of water. The West India Docks were once lined with magnificent Georgian warehouses, an unbroken façade stretching for two-thirds of a mile. Many of these were destroyed in the last war, but some 600-feet frontage at the Western end are still standing and are listed as buildings of architectural and historic interest.

We are about to enter Greenwich Reach, and all necks are craning for a first glimpse of the Naval College. But we have first to pass through the dreary corridor between Millwall and Deptford. The ship brings us close to the Millwall shore and to the now disused entrance to the Millwall Docks; when the Millwall Docks were linked by water to the rest of the West India Docks it was found more convenient to enter from that direction rather than go the longer way round the Isle of Dogs; the Millwall entrance fell out of use and after it was damaged in the last war it was closed permanently. A little below the dock entrance is the site of the building of the leviathan the *Great Eastern*. It is as though someone thought that as the present is so uninspiring we might as well draw inspiration from the past, for the river wall here carries a huge sign which reads: "Site of Building and Launching of Steamship Great Eastern 1853–8. Length 692 feet. 27,384 tons." What a magnificent failure she was, the *Great Eastern*. Bad luck dogged Isambard Brunel, as it had done Marc Brunel his father over the tunnel project, and the crowning irony came when he tried to launch her. Such a great ship could not be launched in the conventional way, instead she had to be launched sideways, but when the time came she stuck. For three months she remained ignominiously stranded like a great whale, whilst the steamship companies made fortunes running trips to see her. She failed as a passenger ship, but served a useful career as a cable-layer. But she ended her days as ignominiously as she had begun them—as a floating fun-fair and outsize advertising gimmick. It was a hard fate for a vessel that had pioneered many new developments later to be widely adopted.

Modern Deptford's mean industrial muddle is a distraction from its fascinating history, so we will close our eyes and see the Deptford of past centuries; with luck we shall be at Greenwich before we have finished with Deptford Past. In selecting Deptford for the site of the Royal Naval Victualling Yard it is just possible that Henry VIII was following in the footsteps of Alfred the Great hundreds of years before. But 1513 is early enough to begin the 450 years of Deptford's history. Queen Elizabeth naturally chose her Royal Dockyard as the setting for her bestowal of knighthood on Sir Francis Drake in 1581, just as Queen Elizabeth II chose Greenwich as the venue for the knighting of another Francis in 1967—Sir Francis Chichester. There the parallel ends. The *Golden Hind* lay anchored in the river with £10 million aboard; the *Gypsy Moth IV* had only a few tins of corned beef. Deptford Creek, where the Ravensbourne enters the Thames, provided a sheltered inlet for shipbuilding, whilst above Deptford the Thames shallows until the Lower and Upper Pool are reached, thus Deptford was a particularly convenient place for the building of the larger ships. Because of this the East India Company built some of their early ships here, but most of the ships built at Deptford were warships. As the size of ships increased Deptford declined as a shipbuilding yard and the Royal Dockyard was closed in 1869. Two years later the site began a curious new career as the Corporation of London's Foreign Cattle Market. This was established after a series of disastrous outbreaks of cattle disease had convinced the Government that the free sale of imported cattle "on the hoof" should be prohibited, and that henceforth all live animals should be brought to one place and there slaughtered. The Deptford Foreign Cattle Market served this purpose until 1910, by which time cattle were no longer being imported on the hoof from the Continent. Thanks to refrigeration, most of the country's meat requirements were by then being met by frozen meat imports from the New World.

The stench and heat below decks of the old cattle ships was appalling, in spite of what a contemporary description calls: "two enormous cowls which turn round and round according to the weather". Reporting to the Transit of Animals Committee in 1869, Dr Symonds wrote: "Suffocation of animals is a common occurrence, especially when speed is slackened in coming up the river, the wind sails not acting with the same amount of power. It is difficult to conceive the amount of heat and effluvium existing in the middle and lower decks when the vessel is brought alongside. The men who go down to get out the animals are compelled to divest themselves of all clothing except their trousers to perform the duty. To relieve their breathing they are also compelled to come to the openings in the decks through which the cattle are brought up for being put ashore." Perhaps it was no great loss when the Deptford Foreign Cattle Market closed down in 1914.

We open our eyes and there it is—the Greenwich Royal Naval College. What a splendid sight!—Sir Charles Reilly called it "one of the most sublime sights English architecture affords". It has such poise, such dignity, such perfection of proportion. The captain slows down his engines as we approach the point in the river at right angles to the college. In these days when everything is off-centre the symmetry is breathtaking, it is like an exercise in perspective. And the wonder is that this is not in fact as Wren first planned it. For once his judgement seems to have been at fault. He wanted to pull down the King's House and the Queen's House and build a large structure with a great central dome like St Paul's. But Queen Mary insisted on their preservation, and it was she who laid down that a clearing not less than 115 feet wide should be kept between Queen's House and the river to preserve the view. Wren accepted these provisions and produced this masterpiece of elegant simplicity. It could not be bettered: it has been called the most unaltered view in London.

Unlike Bermondsey, Rotherhithe and Deptford, Greenwich rises steeply from the riverside to the heights of Blackheath with its incomparable views of the river and the city. Greenwich almost selected itself as the site for a royal palace. It was Margaret of Anjou, wife of Henry VI, who first brought it into prominence by building her Palace of Placentia there; Henry VIII was born there; Edward VI died there. In 1664 Charles II started to build a new royal palace there, but only one block was finished when the money ran out. In 1694, in recognition of the navy's great victory at La Hogue two years before, Queen Mary decided to found a hospital for poor seamen equivalent to the Chelsea Hospital for soldiers established by Charles II. She offered the palace at Greenwich for this purpose and so it was that the Greenwich Royal Naval Hospital received its Charter. Greenwich remained a naval hospital until 1869. In 1873 the Royal Naval College moved there from Portsmouth and established what has been called the University of the Navy. Most navy officers pass through the college at some time in their careers and the Painted Hall plays a rich part in naval tradition, as indeed in national life, for state occasions are often held there.

Immediately behind the Naval College is the National Maritime Museum located partially in the Queen's House which once had the main Deptford–Woolwich road running through the middle of it; the road has now been diverted but its original route is marked by a line of colonnades. The Museum houses a unique and increasingly valuable collection of paintings, models and other exhibits related to the sea and is visited by an average of 2,000 people daily.

Perhaps even better known in the world at large than Greenwich Royal Naval College is the Greenwich Observatory, Greenwich Mean Time and the Meridian. The Observatory, built by Charles II, occupied its commanding site in Greenwich Park until the increasing atmospheric pollution necessitated its removal to Hurstmonceaux Castle in Sussex in 1949. The Octagon Room, designed by Christopher Wren and now part of the National Maritime Museum, was where the Meridian Longitude O was established—it was accepted the world over in 1884. The time ball continues to make its ritual drop at 1 o'clock each afternoon.

One cannot take in the view of the college without also being aware of the ship on the land in the foreground—the famous *Cutty Sark*. The college and the clipper seem already inseparable companions. Both continue the long seafaring tradition of Greenwich, which began long before Henry Hudson sailed from here in 1607 to look for a passage across the North Pole to the East. Built in 1869, seven years after that other clipper the *Flying Spur* returned to Hay's Wharf, and sixty-eight years after the first steamship had sailed on the Thames, the *Cutty Sark* was one of the last, and one of the greatest, of the clipper ships. She was used for only a few years on the China tea run, and it was as a wool carrier on the Australian run that she earned her reputation for speed. She was eventually sold to a Portuguese owner in 1895, later finding her way back to the Thames at Greenhithe where she lay for many years near the training ship *Worcester*. She was moved to her present dry dock in 1954 and is now open to the public. The dock was built by Sir Robert McAlpine and Sons on a non-profit basis; the ship was restored to its original condition by Sir Joseph Rawlinson and his staff on a non-profit basis, and she was entirely re-rigged by R. H. Green and Silley Weir on a non-profit basis. That shows what people will do when their imagination is fired. And the public have responded magnificently. Well over two million people have visited the ship. One cannot mention the *Cutty Sark* without paying a tribute to Mr Frank Carr, lately Director of the National Maritime Museum. It was largely his initiative and enthusiasm that brought the project to a successful conclusion; I was delighted to read recently that he now has plans for the possible preservation of Sir Francis Chichester's *Gypsy Moth IV*. The *Cutty Sark* becomes a class-room in the evenings; the Greater London Council run courses for amateur yachtsmen in the ship—surely an inspiring venue. Inside the vessel is the famous collection of figureheads presented by the late Captain Long John Silver. I was privileged to meet this unique personality some years ago and he personally conducted me round his collection when it was housed at Gravesend—he was a great man of the sea. Figureheads have practically died out these days, but some of the modern Norwegian ships still have them.

As the river swings northwards we leave behind the high land of Greenwich and begin the sharp 180 degrees meander round Blackwall Point. This is historic Blackwall Reach. Captain John Smith and his companions set out from here in 1606, in their three tiny ships the *Susan Constant*, *Godspeed* and *Discovery* to found the new colony of Virginia. One of the most memorable experiences I had on a trip to the United States in 1964 was seeing the true-to-scale reproductions of these three ships lying at anchor off the quayside of the reconstructed town of Jamestown, Virginia. It seems incredible that 144 people, women and children among them, spent months aboard these frail little craft where there was

not even room to stand erect between decks. There is a memorial
to the Virginia Settlers near the entrance to the East India Dock.
But Blackwall is mainly associated in history with the East India
Company. The great ships of the company could not advance
fully loaded further up-river than Blackwall in the days before
the river was dredged efficiently, and so here they had to stop and
unload. In a way this was a blessing in disguise, for it meant
that special measures had to be taken to get the goods to the
warehouses where duty was levied. Two systems were used.
Sometimes the goods were landed at Blackwall and taken under
armed guard to the huge Cutler Street warehouse of the company
in the City, and at other times they were unloaded into lighters,
specially covered to protect the valuable cargoes, and taken on
up-river to the Legal Quays or Sufferance Wharves in the Pool.
Unlike the West India Company, which suffered enormous
losses from theft and plunder before the docks were built, the
East India Company was very little affected. The company had
their own fitting-out dock, the Brunswick Dock, at Blackwall,
but this was not licensed to receive dutiable goods and had no
warehouse facilities. The East India Dock was built in 1806 and
was later called the Import Dock, the old Brunswick being named
the Export Dock. The latter was eventually filled in and the site
used for the construction of the Brunswick Electricity Generating
Station in 1951. Now the Import Dock has come to the end of its
useful life and seems likely to close soon as part of the long process
of modernizing London's dock system. Blackwall was also the
site of one of the great shipbuilding yards on the Thames. Here
the renowned "Blackwallers" were built for the East India
Company and other shipowners, and later some of the fast
clippers. Blackwall claims to be one of the oldest active shipyards
in the world.

But Blackwall is probably associated in most Londoners' minds
with the tunnel. Built between 1889 and 1897 it is London's
oldest tunnel for road traffic. I remember as a child travelling
through the tunnel on the old round-topped buses staring
anxiously at the white tiles dripping wet and becoming more and
more convinced that the river was about to burst in at any
moment. Had I known then that the Thames flows in places only
five feet above the roof of the tunnel I might have been even
more alarmed! Today the traffic has become so heavy that a

second tunnel has been built a little to the east of the old one. The old tunnel wriggles its way under the river like a worm—it has at least half a dozen sharpish bends whilst the new Dartford-Purfleet Tunnel goes straight down and up.

This reference to the tunnel reminds me that I have scarcely mentioned the people who live in these riverside areas. Naturally there are no private houses on the riverside itself, the river frontage is too valuable for commercial and industrial use. Indeed for some distance down-river from London Bridge an Elizabethan ordinance forbade the building of private houses on the river bank so that it might be reserved for commerce. However, before the days of mass transit systems people had no choice but to live as near as possible to their jobs, and there are still hundreds of thousands of people living near, and indeed among, the docks of London. On the Isle of Dogs completely new towns had to be built, towns like Millwall, and Cubitt Town established by Sir William Cubitt in 1843. This is Dockland, famed for the lawlessness of its inhabitants in times past, but now rapidly emerging from the ugliness and squalor of those times. There are many fine new blocks of flats in Millwall, and if there were only a few more riverside spaces open to the public like the Island Gardens, with its magnificent view of the Royal Naval College across the water, the Isle of Dogs might not be an unpleasant place in which to live. One of the problems of living in Dockland is communication between one residential area and another across the docks. On the Isle of Dogs this problem has been resolved by the building of a new high-level footbridge linking Limehouse with Blackwall and passing right across the Millwall Dock. The bridge is forty feet high and access each end is by lift. The section crossing the dock itself can be raised to allow ships to pass underneath; in its raised position it points 140 feet into the sky as if to tell the world that people do count—even in all this babel of commerce. The P.L.A. have spent £250,000 on building this bridge to make living conditions in Dockland more acceptable. It is a pity that the glass used to enclose the bridge is not transparent; if it were the bridge would be a Mecca for photographers.

If we are to encourage people to live on the Isle of Dogs, as we are doing by the building of new blocks of flats, can we not help them to enjoy the island's greatest asset—the river? Londoners' enjoyment of their river is usually passive, they do not

8

swim in it, fish in it, or sail on it. Yet with imagination they could be encouraged to do all these things. A recent report aptly entitled "Londoners Alive" has proposed the building of a swimming pool in the Thames using purified river water—and in the winter it could be frozen and used for skating. Why not indeed? And why do we not cater more specifically for the Londoners' pleasure in river-gazing? Why not provide special viewing platforms so that the activity in the great docks can be enjoyed by the public? Why not indeed? It is as though we are only slowly emerging from a long sleep during which it seemed almost morally wrong for a public authority to make specific provision for people's pleasure: we have become so wedded to the idea of the river as an artery of commerce that we have forgotten its equally traditional role as the focus of recreation for the people.

10

WOOLWICH REACH,
THE ROYAL DOCKS, AND BARKING

Rounding Blackwall Point, the sharpest bend in the tidal river, we enter the oddly named Bugsby's Reach and pass thence into Woolwich Reach. As we pass the entrance to Bow Creek we see the Trinity House Wharf where the many buoys and sea markers round the coast are brought for repair and maintenance. Here, as the saying goes, bad buoys are made good! Below Bow Creek was once a shipyard where battleships were made out of London's scrap iron. It was called the Thames Ironworks and was closed down after the dreadnought *Thunderer* had been launched in 1912. The Thames shipyards could not compete with those in the north of England, and in Scotland, where coal and iron were in close proximity. The *Thunderer* was the last ship of any size to be built on the Thames.[1]

In Woolwich Reach the river plays some odd tricks. In places it is unusually deep, and in others unusually shallow. On the north side of the river lies the notorious Ham Shelf stretching more than half way across the river. It was partly the navigational difficulty caused by this great shoal that led Henry VIII to establish a dockyard at Woolwich as well as the one at Deptford further upstream. He dare not go too far down the river for fear of damage by sudden enemy attack (he did in fact establish another at Erith, but this did not survive for long because of navigational difficulties in this part of the river); however, Woolwich was safe

---

[1] There has recently been a suggestion that the *Warrior*, Britain's first iron-clad battleship, built by the Thames Ironworks in 1860 and at present used as an oil jetty in Pembroke Dock, should be restored and found a permanent berth at the new town of Thamesmead below Woolwich. It will come as no surprise that the moving spirit behind this idea is the same Mr Frank Carr who was primarily responsible for bringing the *Cutty Sark* to Greenwich.

enough, and it lay on the right side of the Ham Shelf. One has to remember that the dockyard was intended for warships, and these were very much larger than other vessels afloat at that time. The famous *Henri Grace à Dieu* launched in 1515 at Woolwich was 1,500 tons, far and away the largest ship afloat at the time; incredible as it seems, it was another two-and-a-half centuries before a ship larger than this was built. No wonder it created a deep impression. From Henry VIII's time onwards a sufficient depth of water was maintained off Woolwich to keep the dockyard in operation, but above Woolwich the navigational channel was reduced by the Ham Shelf to a width of only a few yards. It was because of these difficulties that the Woolwich Dockyard tended to supersede that at Deptford. The Woolwich Dockyard was still building battleships as late as 1854, but Deptford by then had been reduced to corvettes. No vessel of any size could leave the Woolwich moorings to move up-river unless it could make the "holes" off Blackwall or Deptford. The big East Indiamen never went beyond Deptford; there would have been sufficient water in the Pool, but that would have meant negotiating the difficult and shallow Limehouse Reach and the chances were that the Pool would be dangerously crowded on arrival. These are the kind of considerations that the river pilots have had to weigh up over the centuries and still do today. They cannot relax until their charges have been safely handed over to the dock pilot (or "mud" pilot as he is often called) at the dock entrance.

Woolwich today has little of its old nautical flavour. The people cannot get within sniffing distance of their river except in one or two places—out of several miles of waterfront there are only a few yards available to the public. The Royal Arsenal occupies the river front eastwards from the Free Ferry terminal, and the old dockyard monopolizes it on the western side. The last ship was launched there nearly a century ago, and in 1869 most of it was transferred to the War Department for stores and officers' quarters. Its present use has virtually no connection with the river, yet still it robs the people of Woolwich of access to their river. The odd feature of Woolwich is that ever since the Norman Conquest it included a small piece of land on the north bank of the river, the only London borough on the south bank to do so. It was this that gave rise to the saying: "More wealth passes through

Woolwich than any other town in the world." In 1965, when Woolwich was absorbed into the new London Borough of Greenwich the detached portion on the north shore was merged with the new London Borough of Newham. Access to the north shore can be through the pedestrian subway, or by the Free Ferry. The Free Ferry was established in 1889, continuing a tradition dating from at least 1308, and it is operated by the Greater London Council. The old paddle steamers of the Woolwich Free Ferry, which were scrapped in 1963, were almost a legend in their own time, with their thin funnels and almost-circular hulls, and their peculiar crab-like motion. The new boats, with their yellow and cream markings, may be less remarkable than the old, but they do add a welcome splash of colour. Their names are reminders of three great Thameside personalities, John Burns, Ernest Bevin and James Newman. Two boats are kept constantly in use, whilst a third is usually being overhauled on the rather ingenious "dry dock" on the Woolwich side; this consists simply of a flat wooden platform built into the river on which the ferry boat sits when the tide goes out. The new terminal buildings are more impressive than the ferries. Each comprises a huge concrete frame which supports the roadway as it is lowered on the arrival of the ferry, and there is a control cabin perched high up on one side of the frame. Whilst waiting in the car recently to cross the ferry, I asked my neighbour in the queue what the charge was for taking the car across. I had forgotten for the moment that it was free. But the real price you have to pay is the long wait. It was half an hour before I was able to drive on to the boat—and then there is always the risk that a liner will be passing through the lock into the Royal Docks and you will have to wait another quarter of an hour there. When one remembers that this is supposed to be the link between the South Circular and the North Circular roads such delays are ridiculous. Much as I like ferries, I cannot see why these expensive works were ever built in preference to the tunnel which is still obviously required.

Woolwich Arsenal, one of the oldest and largest establishments of its kind in the world, owed its origins partly to the proximity of the Royal Dockyard, and partly to the abundance of fine moulding sands in the cliffs nearby which have been extensively quarried over the centuries, the material being either used locally or shipped elsewhere. The area was known as the "Rabbit

Warren" and retained the name "The Warren" long after the Arsenal was established in the early eighteenth century. An extensive redevelopment scheme, costing £4 million has just recently been announced to provide the most modern working and storage accommodation for the armed services. It seems that Woolwich's military connections will remain for many years yet.

The desolate Plumstead Marshes below Woolwich, whose very isolation made it the ideal location for an ammunition factory in which 40,000 workers were employed in the last war, will soon be completely transformed into London's newest and most revolutionary new town—Thamesmead. This will be a true river town—designed from the word Go to make the maximum use of its riverside setting. "The river is the most positive element in this difficult site", says the Chairman of the Greater London Council, Sir William Fiske, in a brochure describing the new town, "and the aim is to emphasize this in the Master Plan." The 1,300-acre site will be planned to include a 30-acre lake in the centre, a magnificent river promenade with restaurants overlooking the tideway, and a yacht basin capable of taking 2,000 yachts. Most of the three miles of riverside within the town will be parkland open to the public. At long last the people of South London will be shown what can be done to make a riverside site attractive and exciting.

What can be done for 60,000 people in Thamesmead can be done for the hundreds of thousands who live along the other stretches of London's riverside. Places like Wapping, Bermondsey, Upper Thames Street, Fulham, Wandsworth, and many others are crying out for imaginative treatment of this kind. Thamesmead may be the beginning of a movement to give the river back to the people.

The plan for Thamesmead incorporates a scheme for building a new tunnel under the river to link up with the North Circular Road north of the Royal Docks. The proposal is to excavate a huge trench in the bed of the river and to build in it a rectangular-shaped "tunnel" containing two carriageways for traffic.

One of the difficulties of the Thamesmead site which the Chairman of the Greater London Council may have had in mind is that it lies within a stone's throw of the Southern Outfall works at Crossness. This, together with the Barking Outfall

Works across the river, was part of Bazalgette's scheme to intercept sewage on its way to the Thames and to convey it well away
from the London area. He must have thought that he was
allowing a handsome margin for future growth in selecting
Crossness . . . but not so. New town and sewage works must
learn to live together; and that is not all. There are massive
extensions planned for the Crossness works, and these must be
accommodated as well since the continued development of the
whole of South London depends on them. When they were
first erected, the outfall works merely discharged the sewage into
the river in its crude form. But there were soon many complaints
of sewage lying on mudbanks at low tide and in 1882 the Royal
Commission on Metropolitan Sewage Disposal recommended
that the sewage should be treated before being discharged into
the river. The necessary precipitation works were built at Barking
and Crossness in 1887–95. The volume of sewage effluent flowing
into the river from these two works is greater than that of any
other tributary of the Thames, not excluding even the Medway.

Precipitation led to another problem . . . what to do with the
sewage sludge. Prodigious quantities were produced and it soon
became obvious that the only way to dispose of it was to dump
it out to sea. So a fleet of six vessels was specially built to carry the
sludge out to the Black Deep in the Thames Estuary and there to
dump it. The vessel simply opens its valves and the liquid flows
out, the whole process taking only ten minutes. The ship then
returns for more. These vessels are probably unique in that they
do exactly the same round trip every day of their lives—sixty
miles out to the Black Deep on the ebb tide, dump at slack water
and then sixty miles back again on the flowing tide. The ships are
even designed with engines sufficient to enable them to keep to
this daily schedule with the least expenditure of fuel. When, in
thick fog on September 18th 1965, one of these vessels, the *Sir
Joseph Rawlinson*, was involved in a collision in the estuary and
sank with some loss of life, Londoners were reminded for a brief
instant of the daily opening of its bowels that is so vital to the
city's health.

The time has now come to turn our attention to the north
bank. Here lies the most impressive achievement in the story of
London's port, the Royal Group of Docks, 238 acres—the
largest sheet of enclosed water in the world. We will take a trip

right through these docks. Before the building of the Silvertown Way, which crosses the lock entrance on a fixed bridge, it would have been possible to have entered by the west entrance, sail through the docks and emerge by the Gallions Reach entrance, a distance of three miles. However, the western entrance, the original entrance to the Victoria Dock, is now closed to shipping, although it has recently been reopened again for barge traffic only. We will therefore enter from Gallions Reach at the eastern end.

As we wait for the water to rise in the entrance lock this may be a suitable point at which to recall the history of these great docks. The story begins with the construction of the Victoria Dock in 1855, the first dock to have direct rail communications inland. The site was what planners call a "green field" site, that is, it was entirely undeveloped. In fact the land was purchased for its agricultural value, and the land south of the dock was left in pasture in the expectation that it would be used for cattle imported by sea before being shipped to slaughterhouses elsewhere. In the event, however, as we saw earlier, the live cattle trade became centralized at Deptford and these plans did not materialize. The Victoria Dock had a big disadvantage. Its only entrance lay in Bugsby's Reach, it was a narrow entrance and was on the wrong side of the Ham Shelf. As the draught of vessels continued to increase it became obvious that the new dock would soon become obsolete unless something were done. In 1864 the London and St Katharine Docks Company acquired the Victoria Dock because their own docks further upstream were becoming even more out of date and they needed opportunities for expansion downstream. They decided to build a new dock eastwards of the Victoria Dock to provide access to the Thames in Gallions Reach. In 1880 this objective was realized with the opening of the Royal Albert Dock (the Victoria Dock also gained the prefix "Royal" at this time). Both docks could now cater for larger vessels than had previously been able to use the Victoria Dock; but still the draught of vessels increased and it seemed for a time that both docks might become obsolete, and that Tilbury, opened in 1886 to draw traffic from the Royal Group, might indeed succeed in capturing the bulk of the traffic. However, the establishment of the P.L.A. gave a new stimulus to dredging and the dock systems further up the river all received a new lease of life. It now became

The Prospect of Whitby
Outward Bound—West India Docks (overleaf)

a practical proposition to build a new and larger dock to accommodate larger ships as part of the Royal Group. A new deeper lock was built in Gallions Reach, and in 1921 the new King George V Dock was finally opened, after work on it had started before the 1914-18 War. It is into this dock that we now pass from the entrance lock which, incidentally, is 800 feet long, 100 feet wide and 45 feet deep, just big enough to take the *Mauretania* (36,655 tons) which used the lock in 1939, the biggest ship ever to do so. Normally, however, the vessels using the Royal Docks are seldom more than 30,000 tons. We are now at a level two feet above the Thames High Water level as we leave the lock.

Immediately before us lies King George V Dock. It is unusual in having seven "dolphins" along its south side; these are jetties running parallel with the dockside and 32 feet from it, each jetty being 520 feet long. These enable lighters to be loaded on both sides of a ship simultaneously. As we move along the dock we see ships belonging to such famous lines as the Blue Star, Royal Mail and the "Ben" Line. They bring a great variety of goods, but especially grain and tobacco. At the far end of the dock is the massive King George V Dry Dock, 750 feet long and 100 feet wide. We may be lucky and see somewhere about here the P.L.A.'s huge floating derrick "London Mammoth" of 200-ton capacity; she can lift railway engines, coaches, and even small ships into the vessels waiting to receive them. The King George V Dock is the only complete dock designed and built by the P.L.A., but the Authority is building the new container dock at Tilbury.

We now move through the connecting channel into the Royal Albert Dock, without doubt the most impressive of all the London docks. This great sheet of water, over a mile long, is more like an inland sea than an enclosed dock. It has two lock entrances from Gallions Reach, the older and shallower one being 550 feet long 80 feet wide and 30 feet deep, and the newer one, built to meet the challenge of Tilbury, the same length but with a depth of 36 feet. Vessels longer than 550 feet can enter via the King George V Dock. Moving down the Royal Albert Dock and gazing at the names of the long line of ships on either side is one of the great experiences still in store for anyone who has not yet taken a trip through these docks. The low single-storey transit sheds which line the dockside make the ships seem even larger in proportion. Towards the west end of the dock are the two dry

Gateway to the Royal Docks (preceding page)
The ship in the street—Cutty Sark

docks and the ship repairing plants of Harland and Wolff Limited, and R. H. Green and Silley Weir.

Passing through into the Royal Victoria Dock we see at once, dominating the skyline, the tall grain silos and mills on the south side. Grain is one of the most important cargoes handled in this dock. No 8 Shed, Royal Victoria Dock, houses the P.L.A.'s tidal models of the River Thames; the largest is 400 feet long and 44 feet wide, and it has been used extensively to investigate the problems of flooding and the effect of a Thames Barrage. Behind the transit sheds on the north side are the most extensive railway sidings of any dock in Britain. The flat land north and east of here is all owned by the Port of London Authority and might one day be developed for another dock running parallel with the Royal Albert. If we had time we might leave our ship here and visit the large Missions to Seamen hostel in Victoria Dock Road on the other side of the railway tracks and join some of the hundreds of seamen of all nationalities who come for a few hours' recreation and a night's rest in comparative luxury before going off to sea again. One sees seamen of all nationalities there, I know of no more cosmopolitan community in all London. We might see the M.V. *John Ashley*, a floating church and seaman's club run by the mission for the men of the coasters and colliers of the port; she covers about 6,000 miles a year visiting seamen afloat. I believe the German seamen call her the "Blue Angel". So we end our tour of these great docks on this human note. For after all the end purpose of all this enterprise is the greater happiness of mankind, and that includes those who bring these goods to our shores from all the corners of the earth.

We return now to Gallions Reach, a name that recalls one of the greatest tragedies that has ever occurred on the Thames. On a dark night in September, 1878, the *Princess Alice*, a small paddle steamer carrying over 700 passengers back to London from the resort towns of the estuary, and the Rosherville Pleasure Gardens at Gravesend, was hit amidships by the collier *Bywell Castle* in mid-stream and sank within minutes. The life-saving equipment comprised twelve lifebuoys and three boats, but in any case there was no time to escape—the ship had been so badly constructed in an effort to cram in more passengers that she broke in two and sank like a stone. All but a few of the passengers perished. Gavin Thurston wrote a book about this incident, published in 1966, called *The Great Thames Disaster*. So we press on down Gallions Reach, a name said to relate to the Venetian galleys that used to visit London at one time, passing on our left the Beckton Gas Works, one of the largest gas works in the world devouring about 5,000 tons of coal a day, and the Northern Outfall Works, until we come to the mouth of the River Roding and Barking Reach.

Strange as it may seem today, Barking is reputed to be the oldest fishing port in the United Kingdom, and for a short-lived period in the eighteenth and nineteenth centuries it was a major deep-sea fishing port for London. The Barking fishermen made history in 1406 by resisting the seizure of their nets; they were a prickly lot these Barking fishermen; only a few years before they had joined forces with the discontented fishermen of the other Thameside villages of Fobbing and Corringham and so helped to foment the Peasants' Revolt. The key to the rise of Barking as a deep-sea fishing port was the invention of that curious vessel the "welled smack". This had a compartment in the middle, called the "well", which was so constructed that water flowed in and out through holes drilled in the bottom. By this means the fish were kept fresh until the vessel arrived at Billingsgate—this was of course in the days before ice was used. Defoe, in the early eighteenth century, described Barking as " . . . a large town chiefly inhabited by fishermen whose smacks ride in the Thames at the mouth of the river [i.e. the Roding] from whence the fish is sent up to Billingsgate by small boats". Thanks to the welled smack Barking became the most important fishing port in the United Kingdom and one of the most important in the world at this time. In 1814 there were seventy vessels of forty to fifty tons registered in the town, each carrying eight to ten men and boys, and by the middle of the century the number of vessels had risen to 200. The whole town of Barking was given over to the needs of this industry, it was a bustling seaport steeped in the characteristic smells of pitch, tar, and fish.

By their own resourcefulness, however, the Barking fishermen had hastened the eclipse of the town as a fishing port. In 1848 the Barking men were the first to develop the method of packing fish between layers of ice in boxes called "trunks" as a means of preserving them, and the first artificial ice plant in England was installed there. This was followed by the introduction of the fast steam cutter to bring the trunks quickly to Billingsgate. Within a few years these two developments, coupled with the rapid growth in railway transport brought the Barking fishing industry to a sudden close. In 1865 the fishing transferred to Lowestoft and Yarmouth. Barking's brief reign was over—killed, one might say, by the curious combination of ice and steam.

II

HALFWAY REACH
TO NORTHFLEET HOPE

A century ago Barking marked the eastern edge of the Port of London. Between Barking and Gravesend the river, for the best part of thirteen miles, ran between desolate marshes; the only sign of habitation was an occasional farm or riverside pub, like the now vanished "Halfway House" which took its name from the Reach on which it stood. Here and there were small riverside towns situated either on a chalk bluff, like Purfleet and Grays on the north bank and Erith, Greenhithe and Northfleet on the south, or at river crossings like Crayford and Dartford, when they were some distance back from the river. These little towns had some river traffic of their own in such cargoes as coal or timber, but mostly the shipping on the river passed them by *en route* to the Port of London. From the navigational point of view this was a somewhat negative stretch of river. Apart from a tricky patch at Erith Rands, the pilot who boarded the incoming ship at Gravesend could relax for this part of the journey as there was usually sufficient depth of water for all but the largest ships at most states of the tide.

After about 1850 the situation began to change. The Port of London began to reach this part of the river in the course of its expansion eastwards. The process began with the development of Thameshaven in 1853 as a railhead for the landing of live cattle. Then came the building of Tilbury Docks in 1886 (if this had not happened there were already plans for a new dock system at Dagenham), and this stretch of river, linking the two sections of the port, suddenly became very important for the growth of industry. The flat marshland areas lining the river were attractive sites for industrialists looking for riverside access and plenty of space in which to develop. Today this thirteen-mile stretch of river is highly industrialized and is fully as much part of the port as any other part between Teddington and the sea.

Before the advent of the railways and motor-cars this stretch of river was one of the main highways for travellers *en route* to Kent and the Continent. The common practice was to take what was called the "Long Ferry" from London down to Gravesend, and thence travel overland to Dover. The history of the Long Ferry dates back certainly to 1401 if not before. In that year the citizens of Gravesend received a royal charter giving them the monopoly of ferrying passengers to and from London; this was in recognition of the hardships they had suffered in 1377 when a French fleet had sailed up the estuary and sacked their town. Passengers could board a tilt boat or wherry and make the journey usually in one tide.

The Long Ferry was in danger of disappearing in face of the competition of the stage coaches when it was given a temporary reprieve by the introduction of the new steamships in 1815. In the early days they seem to have spent as much time undergoing repairs as in service, but they eventually overcame the teething troubles and were immensely successful. The number of people travelling down-river to Gravesend and back rapidly increased. In 1821 the number of passengers landed at Gravesend pier was 27,000; by 1835 this had risen to 670,452 and eight vessels of the Gravesend Steam Packet Company made a total of 734 voyages to Gravesend and Southend from London, whilst the seven vessels of the Diamond Steam Packet Company made a total of 2,280 voyages to Gravesend. In addition there were another seventeen steamships plying regularly between London and the estuary towns. By 1845 the number of passengers landing at Gravesend had risen to the extraordinary total of 1¾ million. This was the hey-day of the passenger steamers in the lower river. The empty thirteen miles was suddenly a highway along which ran a ceaseless flow of passengers enjoying the still relatively new sensation of steamship travel. Gravesend developed rapidly as a seaside, or rather riverside, watering place. The famous Rosherville Gardens, near Gravesend, opened in 1837. Named after a local resident, Jeremiah Rosher, these offered a wide range of attractions from quiet lawns and archery butts to firework displays to amuse the millions of people who landed from the river steamers, or came by rail on the newly built North Kent line. It was the "Cremorne" of South East London, and indeed outlived its Chelsea equivalent by a few years. The arrival of the railway in the estuary towns broke the steamship boom almost as suddenly as it had started. By 1849 the railway had reached Woolwich, Gravesend and Rochester. The steamship boom was over. Steamships continued to sail on the river, such as the *Princess Alice*, but the railway had taken the impetus out of the steamship traffic. No longer would startled observers see steamships of rival companies racing each other side by side to prove that they were faster than their competitors, the combined wash causing untold havoc. The Long Ferry, as a regular service between Gravesend and London, died in the mid-nineteenth century.

Railways and motor-cars may have killed the Long Ferry, but they brought into being the largest single industrial enterprise on this stretch of the river—the Ford Motor Works at Dagenham. Had it not been for the Tilbury Docks, and the deepening of the river which made the King George V Dock a practical proposition, Dagenham might have become the sixth dock system in London. The site has considerable natural advantages, and these were not lost on Henry Ford when he was looking around Europe for a site that would replicate the advantages of the River Rouge site in Detroit . . . riverside access, plenty of space and a supply of labour nearby. The Dagenham Industrial Estate Company had acquired the site as far back as 1886 and they had raised the level of the marshes to the height of the sea wall by having spoil from the excavations for the London Underground dumped there. Thus the Ford Motor Works, established in 1928, is in a sense built on the London Underground! Even so the site could not bear the enormous weight of a blast furnace (the first and only one in the South of England) and other buildings without extensive piling—in all some 22,000 piles had to be sunk. The blast furnace has the unlikely name Josephine II after the daughter of the late Henry Ford; Fords are the only motor manufacturers in Europe who have their own blast furnace. Sailors have always been grateful for it because the glow acts as a useful guide on foggy nights. The Ford factory also has its own electricity generating station capable of generating sufficient power to meet the requirements of a town of 350,000 people. This is the building that carries the huge Ford sign so familiar to all Thamesmen. A special wharf had to be built out into the river to enable the larger vessels to discharge their supplies of ore and coal, and to load the finished products. There had been a serious breach in the sea wall at Dagenham in 1707 and it was many years before this was eventually sealed. There is still a lake behind the Ford works. As a result there had built up a bad shoal at this point in the river and this was a disadvantage from the point of view of river access. The Dagenham Wharf is the largest private wharf in Britain and is capable of taking ships of 10,500 tons. A different ship comes alongside every three hours on average. In 1965 it exported nearly 60,000 built-up vehicles, and imported over 600,000 tons of coal and 323,000 tons of iron ore. The Dagenham plant produces about 1,500 vehicles every day, and employs 30,000 workers.

In addition to the motor works there is in fact a small dock at Dagenham operated by the Dagenham Industrial Estate Company. A number of firms engaged in storing coal, oil or molasses are located here. Some have built jetties into the river to enable vessels of up to 32,000 tons to come alongside. The riverside here is dominated by two huge 487-foot pylons that carry electric cables across the river.

A power cable can cross at 487 feet without difficulty, but cars and people cannot. The need for a river crossing to supplement the obsolescent ferries at Woolwich and Tilbury grew rapidly as the riverside on both banks became more intensively developed. In 1938 a pilot tunnel of 12 feet diameter was completed between Dartford and Purfleet, but then the war intervened. In 1957 work was resumed and the main tunnel was built, absorbing the smaller tunnel in the process. The main tunnel is 28 feet in diameter and carries a two-lane highway 100 feet below high water in the river. The tunnel was opened in 1963 and will eventually form an important link between the North Orbital and the South Orbital roads, when these have been built. These are now badly needed as the traffic congestion at both ends of the tunnel is serious, especially on the Dartford side. The tunnel's general manager Mr F. L. Millns, in his report for 1966, has referred to queues lasting for several hours at the tunnel approaches during holiday weekends, whilst one motoring journal recently commented on the lack of suitable approach roads and went on to say: "The Forth Bridge with its fine approach roads makes sense, the Dartford Tunnel merely makes nonsense"—a harsh judgement but the point is made. I went out of my way recently to go through the tunnel to get a photograph for this book. As I emerged from the northern end I was pleased to find a service road where I could safely leave my car for a few minutes and I walked back to the tunnel entrance to take the photograph. As I was taking it a policeman came running up and said that photographs were not allowed. He pointed to an object immediately ahead and said this was a television camera which enabled the tunnel supervisor to see all that was happening. Why should I not be allowed, indeed encouraged, to take a photograph of Britain's latest tunnel? In the United States there would be a special platform incorporated into the general design to facilitate this . . . but in our country it is a crime. Surely we have a lesson to learn in public relations somewhere along the line. At least we are a little ahead of the Russians—they didn't confiscate my camera!

Near the north end of the tunnel lies Purfleet, at a point where a ridge of chalk crosses the river at Erith Rands, runs along the north bank as far as East Tilbury, and then recrosses at the Lower Hope to emerge again at the appropriately named village of Cliffe. It is significant that at the two places where this ridge crosses the river, Erith Rands and the Lower Hope, there have always been navigational difficulties due to inadequate depth of water. Chalk has been quarried at Purfleet for hundreds of years. Old leases of chalk pits at Purfleet dated 1574 and 1594 have been found which carried obligations to deliver chalk annually between April and June for the river walls of West Thurrock "according to th'olde custome". Chalk was widely used for strengthening the river walls before the eighteenth century when Kentish ragstone came into use for this purpose. Chalk is still used on the walls today. Following the 1953 floods about one million cubic yards of chalk were used on the North Kent walls alone. Chalk was also used in time past for spreading on the clay soils to improve their friability and fertility, and a substantial trade developed in the sale of chalk from the riverside quarries to farming areas in South Essex and North Kent. Today, however, by far the most important use for chalk is in cement making. Cement is basically a mixture of chalk and clay with gypsum added, the mixture being fused together in a furnace. Thus a riverside location, where chalk and clay are found in juxtaposition and where coal and gypsum can be imported by sea, is the most

9

desirable. The Thameside chalk quarries satisfy these requirements, and after William Aspdin had invented Portland Cement
at Northfleet the Thameside area rapidly became one of the most
important cement producing centres in the United Kingdom.
With large cement works at Purfleet, Swanscombe, Grays, Erith
and Cliffe the Thames region produces about half the total cement
output of the United Kingdom. The longer-established quarries
have grown so large that in places they have completely altered
the natural landscape. A road runs along a narrow neck of land
between two deep quarries connected by tunnel; houses are
perched on the edges of steep 100-feet cliffs (there is a good
example immediately you emerge from the northern end of the
Dartford-Purfleet Tunnel); a cement-making plant occupies the
worked out floor of an old quarry so that the chalk from a nearby
pit can be fed to the works by gravity whilst clay can be brought
in by river at ground level . . . and there is a thin film of white
dust on the allotment cabbages.

Purfleet is also an important oil depot. As you enter the town
from the east you pass so many oil tanks that you begin to feel
positively oily. Purfleet must be the oiliest town on the Thames.
There is more oil at Thameshaven, but that is not a town, it is
one great oil refinery. In the early days of petroleum imports into
London there were a number of serious explosions and fires, and
the authorities became so alarmed that the Petroleum Act of 1871
was passed by which ships laden with petroleum were forbidden
to proceed up-river above Thameshaven. However, in time people
became more familiar with petroleum, and learned how to handle
it safely, and there was considerable pressure on the part of river
interests above Thameshaven to have the limit moved further
up-river. Eventually in 1938 the limit was removed to Crayford-
ness near Purfleet and ever since then Purfleet has been an important oil port. Tankers of more than 30,000 tons cannot reach
Purfleet fully loaded, although not long ago a tanker of 50,000
tons arrived at Purfleet after discharging part of its oil at Thameshaven. The small tankers bring over 1½ million tons of petroleum
and petroleum products to Purfleet each year. There are no
refineries, but only oil storage installations, for vegetable oils as
well as petroleum. Before we leave Purfleet we must dispose of
the old myth that the town derived its name from Queen
Elizabeth's comment when she climbed a local hill to review her

fleet before it set out to meet the Armada and exclaimed: "Oh, my poor fleet!" This is of course nonsense since the town's name figures on documents dating back to the twelfth century. One local historian has dryly commented that after climbing the hill Queen Bess probably said, "My poor feet!"

Dartford, at the other end of the tunnel, is an old river-crossing town on the River Darent with a fine roofed-in galleried inn, the Royal Victoria and Bull, which is a fitting reminder of the town's ancient history as a staging point on the old Dover Road. Dartford has still very much the air of a country town, despite the heavy industrialization of the last hundred years. The town was the earliest centre for paper-making, perhaps the second most characteristic industry after cement of the thirteen miles between the docks. Sir John Spilman, whose tomb is located in the church by the riverside, came from Lindau on Lake Constance and built at Bicknors, Dartford, the first commercially successful paper mill in England in 1588. The word "foolscap" is said to have been derived from the jester in the family arms that Sir John used as a watermark. Today there are paper and board mills at Dartford, Swanscombe, Northfleet, Purfleet and Gravesend, as well as those on the Medway and Swale.

This chapter threatens to become a lecture in the geography of the Lower Thames, so I will pass lightly over the many other activities going on along these thirteen miles, its power stations, explosive factories and stores, sewage works, isolation hospitals, military establishments and land reclamation works . . . and instead we will take a walk along the old High Street of Greenhithe. You approach along a peaceful narrow by-way of a road, and the High Street, which is a High Street in name only for there is little traffic, only one or two friendly little shops and the indefinable atmosphere of ships and the sea, leads down to the river's edge. You pass the busy Everard Shipyard, turn the corner and there, moored only a stone's throw from the shore is the Thames Nautical Training College ship *Worcester*, a steel ship built in 1905 in the style of an eighteenth-century ship of the line and glistening black and white in the sharp June sun. After the *Cutty Sark*, which shared this station in the river with her for so many years, she is probably the most photographed ship on the River Thames. However, in September 1968 a new training college will open in Greenhithe, using some of the *Worcester*'s facilities and whether she will then continue to grace this part of the river in the years ahead is in doubt.

Broadness Point, near Greenhithe, was the scene a few years ago of the sinking of the *Magdeburg*. At 2 o'clock on the morning of October 27th 1964, the M.V. *Magdeburg* (6,629 g.r.t.), carrying 1,900 tons of cargo and 42 omnibuses intended for Cuba, was in collision with the *Yamashiko Maru* and sank in shallow water. For many months she lay on her side in the river, fortunately away from the main fairway, and was raised by the P.L.A. engineers in the summer of 1965. She was taken to Tilbury Docks for hull repairs. The story had a sad ending because she sank in a storm off Ushant whilst being towed to the Piraeus.

Northfleet developed a shipbuilding industry in 1778 as part of the seaward migration of the Port of London. In that year, a shipbuilder named Thomas Pitcher who owned a shipyard near Blackwall, realizing that the size of vessels would increase, decided to move down-river to where the river was deeper and wider than at Blackwall. He acquired a derelict chalk quarry at Northfleet and built a shipyard there. Some East Indiamen and many warships were built here before the dockyard closed down in 1857. There were many subsequent schemes for reopening the dockyard, but these came to nothing and today the site is occupied by Bowaters paper mill erected in 1926 and one of the world's largest paper plants.

On the north bank lies the historic and sizeable town of Grays. Before Tilbury was built Grays was the first town on the north bank of the river and it enjoyed considerable importance as a port of call for coastal vessels. The town is the headquarters of the Thurrock Urban District, one of the largest in Britain, and if the magnificent new swimming pool and civic hall, and Thurrock's excellent parks, are anything to go by, it is also one of the most progressive. Grays has a busy main street that runs at right angles to the river and peters out quite unexpectedly beyond the level crossing. More than once I have followed the main street thinking it was the main road along the river bank, only to find my retreat cut off by the level crossing.

We end this chapter on a note of mystery. Near Grays is a triangular piece of woodland, alongside the main road to Southend, which is called Hangman's Wood. Near the centre of the wood is a high wire fence; it protects the entrance to one of the most extensive areas of dene holes in Britain. Space will not permit me to discuss the fascinating problem of dene holes, which are very numerous on Thameside, but the most commonly accepted explanation these days is that they were excavations for chalk. But exactly why they had to dig as many as forty of these inter-communicating caverns, shaped like vases with narrow necks, below the surface must remain a mystery. Some years ago when I was exploring the area I arrived at Hangman's Wood just as a team of cave-diving enthusiasts were making an examination of the holes. In vain I tried to persuade them to let me go down—they obviously thought this was no place for the amateur speleologist. So I have never seen them at close quarters, but as I speed along the road to Southend I am down there among the flotsam and jetsam of past centuries, some of it dating back to Roman times, wallowing in the mystery.

12

TILBURY AND GRAVESEND—
GATEWAY TO THE PORT

Gravesend is the historic gateway to London; it is the first place where the narrowing river impinges upon high land. In 1840 there was even an attempt, happily unsuccessful, to change the name of the town to "Firstport". Below Gravesend the Thames flows between extensive marsh flats on either side, protected by a high sea wall, but here it meets the "land" and the sea wall disappears for a while, to reappear again on the other side of the town. Here is London's natural doorstep, where in Tudor times it was customary for the high dignitaries of the realm to meet distinguished visitors from abroad. We will land at Gravesend and take the steep climb up Windmill Hill, 200 feet above sea level, for the sake of the magnificent panorama of Tilbury and Gravesend the twin portals of the Gateway to the Port.

Immediately below us lies Gravesend Town, the town of the steamship boom, rows of dignified Victorian streets clothing the lower slopes of the hill and away from the more raucous seaport neighbourhood down by the river. Beyond lie the old weather-board inns and the jumble of narrow streets climbing steeply from the river, and in the middle St George's Chapel of Unity in which lies the memorial to Princess Pocohontas the Indian Princess who died in Gravesend in 1616 on her way back to America . . . it soars above the surrounding roofs loudly proclaiming that Gravesend was a seaport long before the steamships first arrived. The old town is clustered round three piers projecting into the river, the West Pier, from which the car ferries *Mimie* and *Tessa* used to ply backwards and forwards across to Tilbury until December 1964 when the service was withdrawn following the opening of the Dartford Purfleet tunnel; the Town Pier from which the passenger ferry to Tilbury continues to run (the "Short Ferry" as it was called to distinguish it from the "Long Ferry"); and the Royal Terrace Pier, headquarters of the London Pilotage Service.

For many years now, all ships entering the Thames have been obliged to have a pilot on board, and the pilotage service is one of the services administered by the Corporation of Trinity House. Ships entering the Thames Estuary have to take on board a "sea pilot" far out to sea, off the Sunk Light Vessel near Harwich for vessels approaching by the northern channel, or off Dungeness or Dover if they are approaching by the southern channel. The sea pilot brings the ship to Gravesend where he hands over to the river pilot who takes the ship up to the dock entrance; there he hands over to the dock pilot who is responsible for the ship in the dock. There are over 500 pilots licensed by Trinity House for the Thames area alone, including both sea pilots and river pilots, and Gravesend runs the largest pilot station in the world. They come under the charge of the oddly named "Ruler of Pilots", a title dating from the times when pilots were an independent and some-what unruly breed of men! Gravesend is also the headquarters of the P.L.A. Thames Navigation Service. The specially designed building on the Gravesend waterfront, opened in 1959, houses complicated radar and radio equipment which, together with other installations further downstream, gives full radar coverage from Southend to Northfleet Hope. In dense fogs this is invaluable in helping to keep the port running; on average there are about 237 hours of dense fog in the river every year. About 22,000 ships pass this building inward bound every year. With the assistance of radar the pilot's job is greatly eased; it is still a responsible job, but less hair-raising today than it was in times past when a ship's captain was empowered to strike the head off the pilot who made a mistake! The pilot cutter is a familiar sight in Sea Reach, but in recent years experiments have been made with the use of helicop-ters and it may be that the "pilot 'copter" will replace the cutter in due course. The Germans already use helicopters for this purpose.

Along the riverside of Gravesend are many evidences of the long and eventful history of the port. There is the little church down by Bawley Bay called St Andrew's Waterside Church, but better known as the "Fisherman's Church". The bells were formerly used to ring out the emigrant ships, and the registers contain some 500 baptisms on board ship of the children of emigrants outward bound for Australia. What many scenes of heartbreak must have been witnessed on Gravesend's waterfront as explorers, colonists, transportees and emigrants took their last look at home before the ship stood out to sea. Inside the church is a brass tablet commemorating Canon C. E. R. Robinson who founded the world-wide St Andrew's Waterside Mission to Seamen in 1864. St Andrew's is the only church on Thameside actually built out into the river.

Bawley Bay, an insignificant little harbour to bear such a title, is a reminder of the days when Gravesend was an important fishing port during the nineteenth century. Indeed Gravesend had been a fishing port of some consequence for many hundreds of years before that. It contributed men and ships, for instance, towards the English fleet during the siege of Calais in 1346. But it was in the eighteenth and nineteenth centuries that the town rose to its greatest importance as a fishing port. In 1735 there were thirty-five vessels working for cod alone, and in 1796 there were no less than 120 deep-sea fishing smacks of fifty to sixty tons registered at Gravesend, with at least 1,200 fishermen employed in the industry. The deep-sea fishing fleet declined in the latter part of the nineteenth century, but the shrimping industry took its place. Old photographs show Bawley Bay crowded with the little shrimping vessels called "Bawleys", a boat peculiar to the Thames Estuary. A few years ago there were still a few of these old boats operating from Gravesend (there is a tradition that you never see a new Bawley) but they had been fitted with engines which had given them a new lease of life since they could now operate in all states of weather and tide. I have myself been out in one of the Gravesend shrimpers in the early morning. It is uncanny how the fishermen locate the shrimps; they seem to have a sixth sense. The shrimps are thrown into a cauldron immediately they are caught. It is not very pleasant for the shrimps, but I found the warmth of the coal fire very welcome on a cold winter's morning in Sea Reach. These few boats were the lone survivors of a great tradition that has earned the Gravesend seamen the nickname "Shrimp" over the oceans of the world. Shrimping in the Thames Estuary is still an important industry, but it is now mainly carried on at Leigh-on-Sea and Rochester.

Swinging our gaze a little further downstream we see the

attractive gardens of Gordon Terrace which gives a wonderful view of the shipping in the river and is much appreciated and used by the people of Gravesend. Moored in the river off the Royal Terrace Pier are a number of tugs, these are privately owned and are waiting to be used for ocean-going vessels entering the river. A little further downstream is the floating headquarters of the Port Health Authority, the hulk *Hygeia*, which is kept manned night and day. Every vessel that enters the river has to present a Declaration of Health, and if this is satisfactory a "Free Pratique" is issued by the first Customs officer who visits the ship. Until this has been issued the ship is completely "excommunicated" from the shore. If there is any doubt the medical officers of the Port Health Authority board the ship and make an inspection. If there are any cases of infectious disease aboard there is the Port isolation Hospital on the Denton Marshes where the patients can be accommodated.

The name "Gordon" is indelibly part of Gravesend. General Gordon spent six years in the town (1865-71) where he was put in charge of the new fortifications recommended to be built by the 1860 National Defence Commission. These included several large new forts in the Thames Estuary for the defence of London.

Fresh from his exploits in China, and with such a fiery nature as his, General Gordon did not easily reconcile himself to this task, especially as he regarded the whole scheme as a piece of anachronistic folly. However, he set about the task with great energy and was constantly seen walking rapidly about the new forts supervising the works, or being rowed furiously along the river by four oarsmen who were virtually collapsing from exhaustion after being subjected to a continuous exhortation to "Row a little faster boys, a little faster". The spare energy he had left after his day's work was done he devoted to works of charity in the town. It is strange to think of this national hero, "Chinese Gordon", delivering tracts at street doors, sitting with a paralytic, distributing hundreds of suits each year to the needy, and founding a "ragged school" for the urchins of Gravesend—his beloved "scuttlers" as he called them. I wonder if it is still there, the old building I once came across down by Gravesend's waterfront with a plaque indicating that it was the site of the General's ragged school. In 1871 he was invited by Mr Gladstone to accept a post on the Danubian Commission and he left Gravesend.

Behind him he left something of a legend, and today this has taken tangible form in the fine statue of General Gordon in the Gordon Memorial Gardens. We have not heard the last of General Gordon in this portrait—as we take our bird's eye view of the estuary we shall come across the fruits of his labours in many places.

It was mainly considerations of defence that first caused Gravesend's name to be linked with that of Tilbury. Tilbury is entirely a creation of the nineteenth century. If one looks at Chapman and André's wonderfully detailed map of 1777 there is virtually nothing on the site of Tilbury except a farmhouse or two, Tilbury Fort, and then just uninhabited marsh. The port began life as a small blockhouse erected by Henry VIII in 1538 as part of a defensive scheme to protect the capital and the new dockyards further up-river. This was the obvious site for a defensive position because the river narrows sufficiently at this point to enable land-based cannon to control the river effectively. It is just possible that the sight of the narrowing river and the blockhouses of Gravesend and Tilbury deterred De Ruyter, the Dutch Admiral, from advancing further up the river during his audacious raid of 1667, but it was more likely to have been the problem of negotiating the difficult "S" bend of the Lower Hope if the wind should change, coupled with the lack of adequate space for manœuvre, that caused him to turn back. However, the raid had a salutary effect on British public opinion, probably out of all proportion, in fact, to its military significance. On a wave of public indignation the old blockhouse at Tilbury was pulled down and a large new fort constructed by Bernard de Gomme in 1670–1683 at great expense on account of the marshy nature of the soil. For a long time Tilbury was one of the most important military camps in the country. The fort at Gravesend was also rebuilt at this time. Despite many alarms and excursions, however, especially during the Napoleonic Wars, when ten frigates were stationed across the Lower Hope for two years to protect London from the Napoleonic threat, and again during the "Gordon" period, Tilbury Fort was never called upon to fire a shot in anger. It remains today a magnificent example of the military architecture of its period, carefully restored by the Ministry of Works and opened to the public in 1958.

Tilbury is probably best known in history as the site of the famous review by Queen Elizabeth of her army encamped here under the Earl of Leicester in 1588, ready to repel the Spaniards should the Armada succeed in breaking through the sea defences. However, the site of the camp was not down here by Tilbury Fort, which was altogether too marshy and unhealthy, but a mile or two back from the river around and behind the attractive and unspoiled village of West Tilbury. The army of 17,000 men must have occupied a considerable area. There it was that Queen Elizabeth is said to have uttered the familiar words: "I know I have the body of a weak feeble woman, but I have the heart and stomach of a king, and a king of England too." Even as the review was in progress news was received that the Armada had already been defeated and the remnants were fleeing northwards to escape round the north of Scotland. The little village of West Tilbury was an appropriate setting for this historic scene since it had once before, ten centuries ago, played an important role in history when St Chadd made this his regional headquarters for the evangelizing of the East Saxons. The neighbouring village of Chadwell St Mary is named after him. The settlement founded by St Chadd was called Tilaburg, the town ("burg") at the end ("til") of the road, and it has been suggested that this may have been at East Tilbury rather than West Tilbury.

Present-day Tilbury is by comparison with these stirring chapters of history a very dull town. It would never have been built here at all were it not for the docks which were constructed in 1886. Once the docks had been built it was inevitable, in the pre-car age, that a town would follow for the housing of the workers. If the docks had been built twenty years later it is just conceivable that Tilbury Town might have come into existence on the plateau of West Tilbury, and what a fine location that would be with its extensive views of the estuary. In the Greater London Plan (1944) it was suggested that the whole town should be moved to the vicinity of Grays, but that was in wartime days when such proposals did not seem too visionary. Perhaps Tilbury could be made a more attractive place in which to live if a more imaginative use were made of the many opportunities for water recreation that abound on such a site. Using the old moat of Tilbury Fort for pleasure boating, excellent as this is for the children, simply does not match up to the opportunities.

And so we come to the docks themselves—the sole *raison d'être* for Tilbury. The building of the Tilbury Docks was a far-sighted move that very nearly did not succeed. The basic reasoning was sound enough. The size of vessels was continually increasing, the river channel was becoming increasingly inadequate, and already it seemed that the docks nearer London were becoming obsolete. And anyway, something had to be done to meet the challenge of the Royal Albert Dock completed in 1880, otherwise they would just have to throw in the gauntlet and admit defeat. But what the East and West India Dock Company did not realize was that, faced with this fresh challenge the other dock companies would not tamely submit but would secure such an improvement in the river channel that not only would vessels continue to reach them without difficulty but larger vessels still would come, to new and larger docks. So it was that in the early years of its existence Tilbury Docks was hardly used at all. Its location twenty-six miles downstream from London Bridge, which should have been its great asset was simply a liability. And here another miscalculation was made. Tilbury Docks was intended to be used almost entirely for rail transit; no warehouses were built and it was thought that lighters would not use the docks to any extent because of their distance. In fact, however, it was found that the rail traffic did not materialize as had been expected, whilst after an initial attempt to boycott the new docks on the part of the lightermen they came to be used as much by lighters as any other docks in the port. Another miscalculation was made in the initial costing of the project, which might have been avoided (the miscalculation, not the high cost) if anyone had bothered to read up the history of Tilbury Fort beforehand. No provision was made for the fact that on Tilbury Marshes the alluvial mud is very much thicker than it is near London. The Government had been forced to spend £6,000 on the consolidation of the marsh subsoil with chalk from Northfleet during the building of Tilbury Fort, but this was in Charles II's reign, and the lesson was lost on the Victorians. When they came to build quays for the docks they had to go down as much as seventy feet before they could find suitable bedrock. Even the design of the docks was faulty. A tidal basin was planned so that the dock entrance would be in a sheltered position away from the main tidal stream. What they had not foreseen was that the basin would silt up very quickly and this is exactly what happened. The P.L.A. has to keep a dredger constantly at work keeping the tidal basin clear of mud. It has been estimated that the Tilbury tidal basin accounts for one-seventh of the material dredged from the whole of the Thames each year. Moreover the tidal basin was so designed that it could not readily be enlarged so that an enitrely new dock entrance had to be built in 1929 opening into Northfleet Hope, 1,000 feet long and 110 feet wide, the largest dock entrance in the port. Another miscalculation was the 1,000 feet long cargo jetty built in 1921. This has not been used as much as was expected because of the difficulty of berthing modern liners in a tidal river.

In its early days Tilbury only attracted traffic by offering ridiculously low rates. This exacerbated the vicious rate war between the various dock companies and led eventually to the establishment of the Port of London Authority. Thus good came out of it after all. And in due course the early hopes for Tilbury were fully realized. Tilbury came to be used by the largest vessels sailing from London to India and the Far East, particularly the P & O liners. Major extensions in dock capacity became necessary in 1917, and in 1956. A dry dock, the largest in the port, was added in 1928, and in 1930 the passenger landing stage was opened facilitating direct rail communication with London. Today another large dock extension is under way on the north side of the main dock. This will be the largest container dock in Britain and is expected to be in service from January 1968. The development of containerization, the movement of goods in huge boxes called "containers" rather than loose, has been described by Mr Dudley Perkins, Director-General of the P.L.A. as having as great an impact on the development of international trade as the changeover from sail to steam. Great Britain is far behind the United States in the development of containerization, but the P.L.A. is doing its best to put us back in the race. Another new development at Tilbury is the construction of special jetties to accommodate the drive-on-drive-off services to Antwerp and Rotterdam. Immediately north of the Tilbury Dock Entrance in Northfleet Hope is being built the largest and most modern grain terminal in Britain. It will be capable in due course of taking vessels of up to 45,000 tons, and the silos, towering 225 feet above the Thames marsh, will hold 35,000 tons in the first instance, possibly being increased later to 120,000 tons. Grain will be discharged at the rate of 2,000 tons per hour, as fast as any existing or projected European terminal is capable of achieving. All this is part of London's response to the challenge of Europort. Tilbury, once the Cinderella of London's dock systems, is now in the front line of London's struggle to retain its position among the great ports of the world. The vision of those who decided to move thirteen miles down the river in one great leap has been fully justified, and it may be that vision of an equal sort is now required for another leap downstream in search of deeper water.

PART THREE

TILBURY TO THE TONGUE
THE DEVELOPING ESTUARY

13

INTRODUCING THE ESTUARY

The estuary of the Thames was for centuries a lost forgotten backwater by-passed by the main roads and railways, and inhabited by people who lived in social isolation. Each year many thousands of ships passed through the estuary but saw only a dull, flat and featureless marshland country—none ever stopped to investigate. "We are out of the stream here", wrote the newly arrived rector of Cliffe in his parish magazine in 1881, "and those who drift out of the stream float into a backwater, and the characteristic of a backwater is stagnation." People in the Hundred of Hoo, the large area of land between the Thames and Medway, still repeat the old saying: "The Hundred of Hoo is the last place God made . . . and never finished." A recent book about the estuary carries the apt title *The Unknown Estuary*. There was for centuries, and there is still, an aura of mystery about the flat country of the estuary. "The estuary of the Thames", wrote Joseph Conrad, "is not beautiful, it has no noble features, no romantic grandeur of aspect, no smiling geniality: but it is wide open, spacious, inviting, hospitable at the first glance, with a strange air of mysteriousness which lingers about it to this very day."

Today the Thames Estuary is changing fast; few regions of Britain have undergone a more dramatic transformation. Where there was once nothing but desolate marshland there are now towns like Canvey Island, Coryton and Tilbury; where there was once no employment but farming and a little fishing there are now huge oil refineries employing many thousands; and where once half the people suffered from malaria (or ague, its older name) visitors now come in their thousands to Southend-on-Sea, Westcliff, Canvey and Allhallows to enjoy the health-giving ozone. This is a region in the process of transformation and the process is by no means yet complete; in fact it may be only just beginning.

How did this great change come about? What factors were responsible for lifting the region from a backwater into the main stream of economic development? First must be put the conquest of that old scourge of all the marshland areas of Britain—ague or malaria. Lambarde, writing of the Hundred of Hoo in 1570, says: "Hoo is taken from 'Hoh' in Old English which means Sorrowe or Sickness, a suitable name for this unwholesome

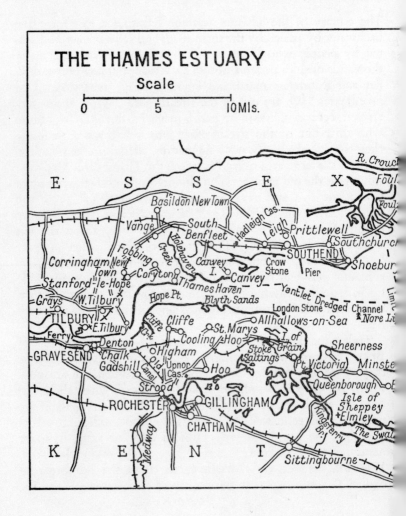

Hundred." His etymology may not have been of the best, but his message is clear. And everyone who visited the marshland areas came away with the same opinion. When Daniel Defoe visited the Essex marshlands in his *Tour Through the Eastern Counties of England* in 1722 he wrote:

I was informed that in the marshes over against Canvey Island there was a farmer who was then living with the five and twentieth wife, and that his son, who was then but 35 years old, had already had about fourteen. The reason, as a merry fellow told me, who said he had had

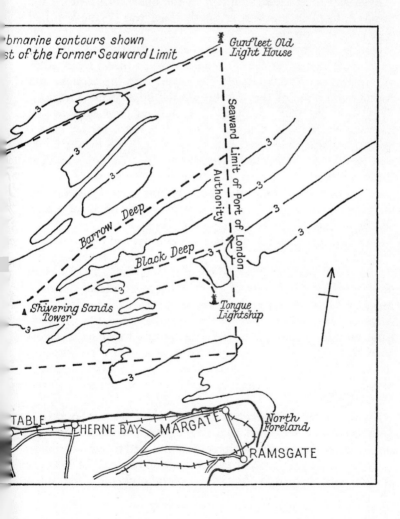

about a dozen and a half wives, was this: that they being bred into the marshes of themselves and seasoned to the place did pretty well with it, but that they always went up into the hilly country . . . for a wife. That when they took the young lasses out of the wholesome and fresh air they were healthy fresh clear and well, but when they came out of their native air into the marshes among the fogs and damps they presently changed their complexion, got an ague or two, and seldom held it above half a year or a year at the most. "And then", said he, "we go to the uplands again and fetch another."

Even as late as the second half of the nineteenth century the common form of greeting in South Essex was "Have you had your ague this spring?"

During the nineteenth century many determined attempts were made to combat the ague, and in 1854 a Select Committee of Parliament was established "To Inquire into the Sanitary and Agricultural State of the Marshes on the sides of the Thames". They reported that adequate land drainage was the answer; stagnant water enabled the anopheles mosquito, carrier of the disease, to breed. Improved drainage, coupled with the introduction of quinine (marshland farmers gave regular doses to their workers during the nineteenth century) finally stamped out the disease. After centuries of subjection to this debilitating scourge the estuary was at last free. The way was now open for a new chapter in this history of the region to begin.

Meanwhile several important developments had taken place in the Estuary which were shortly to bear fruit. Reference has already been made to the construction of Tilbury Docks as an outlying part of the Port of London. An even earlier development, although only a railhead and jetty rather than a dock, was Thameshaven, built in 1855 for the live cattle trade. On the south bank another branch line brought the railway to the jetty at Port Victoria on the Isle of Grain, but this was used for passengers rather than cattle. We shall see how these two developments paved the way for the growth of the great oil refineries in our own time.

Developments of a different kind were taking place at Southend-on-Sea and Canvey Island. Once the ague had been removed the proximity of these riverside sites to London, and the new mobility of people with railways and motor vehicles, made them specially attractive for recreation. As early as 1810 Southend, a few miles

away from the aguish marshes, and with high cliffs giving fine
views of the river, was rapidly becoming a popular watering
place. Progress was relatively slow until the second railway line
reached the town in 1889, and by that time the population had
only increased to about 12,000. From then onwards Southend
grew by leaps and bounds. At the same time Canvey Island was
throwing off three centuries of deep rural isolation and was
attracting holiday-makers, and people looking for somewhere to
retire to, in large numbers. On the south bank the huge area of
mud flats known as the Blyth Sands, and the wide expanse of
reclaimed marsh behind the sea wall, inhibited similar developments, except at Allhallows-on-Sea. Here a narrow tongue of high
land pierces the Hundred's marshland fringe and meets the sea
in an attractive strand. With the building of a branch line here in
1932 it seemed for a moment that the success story of Southend-
on-Sea might be repeated on the south bank, but as we shall see,
these expectations were not fulfilled.

Ague, deep water for ships, the river for recreation; these are
the keys to the development of the estuary. But there is still
another and historically a very important one, its strategic
position astride the entrance to the country's largest port. Since
earliest times the Estuary has been both a valuable protection in
depth to the capital city and its port, and at times, when vigilance
was lowered, a vulnerable sector in the country's defences.
Throughout its history London has escaped the sackings and
destruction that every great city and port on the Continent has
suffered at some time or other. Whilst this was mainly due to
Britain being on an island it was also due to the capital's secure
position fifty miles from the mouth of the river. After the
Norman Conquest no enemy fleet ever reached London along
the river however weak Britain's naval power was at times. But
London could not depend only upon defence in depth—the river
was not only a protection it was also a danger. There was no
easier way to advance directly to the capital than by water. So it
was that throughout the centuries there have been many forts
built at commanding sites on both sides of the estuary, from the
crude earthen blockhouse on the marshes at Higham, that had
collapsed into the river even before De Ruyter appeared in the
Thames, to the curious anti-aircraft forts that were towed out
into the Estuary and lowered on prepared sites on the sea-bed

during the last war. Once again the river was a potential weakness in the capital's defences—there was no easier route to follow on a moonlit night.

So much for our thumb-nail sketch of the developing Estuary. Now we take to the air for our tour of what Charles Dickens: called: "the marsh country down by the river".

14

GRAVESEND REACH
AND THE LOWER HOPE

Of all the reaches of the Thames below London Bridge I like Gravesend Reach best of all. It is a fine piece of water, straight, wide and deep; it makes a magnificent entrance to London River. Here, where the Outer Estuary gives way to the Inner Estuary, hundreds of sailing vessels would be waiting in times past for a favourable wind to round the Lower Hope if outward bound, or to move into the upper river if inward bound. Often a vessel had to wait for days or even weeks for a favourable wind to put to sea, whilst vessels waiting to come into the river would be congregating in the outer estuary waiting for the wind to change. Fishing vessels sometimes had no choice, after waiting several days, but to jettison their catch overboard and make out to sea again. When the wind veered to the right quarter the waiting vessels would crowd on all sail and race each other to be the first to reach the London market, particularly the fishing vessels or the colliers from the North-east. After spells of bad weather the price of coal in London sometimes rose quite high and there were handsome rewards for the ships that arrived first.

However, the City of London had not been slow to take its toll of the lucrative coal trade to the capital. As early as 1306, when London Bridge had been standing for a hundred years and was probably badly in need of repairs because the king had confiscated the bridge revenues, the Mayor and citizens of London were authorized to levy a tax on all coal shipments passing under London Bridge to be used for the maintenance of the bridge. After the Great Fire of 1666 Parliament passed an Act for rebuilding the City of London under which all coal brought into the Port of London became subject to a special tax which was to be collected at Gravesend. It was meant to last for only ten years, but as so often happens with taxes, this one out-lasted many Parliaments. And, as so often happens also, people at once set their minds to the task of finding ways of avoiding the tax. Coal wharves were established at many places below Gravesend, at such places as Mucking Creek, Tilbury Ness (which soon came to be called Coalhouse Point, the name it now bears), Bill Meroy's Creek, and Denton near Gravesend. In old maps the roads to East Tilbury, Tilbury Fort and Denton are all called Coal Road. At Coalhouse Point I have noticed a layer of coal dust about a foot below the surface at the exposed water's edge.

The period 1825–40 was the worst in the river's history from the point of view of congestion. Sometimes several hundred colliers would arrive off Gravesend at the same time, causing immense confusion, as there was at this time no system for allocating berths or controlling the movement of the ships through the lower reaches and into the port. There were several schemes for the building of special docks for colliers, but this was a counsel of despair since the collier wants only to discharge its cargo quickly and then be off again for another load. The introduction of steam colliers which were independent of wind and tide, and the use of new systems of marshalling the colliers, overcame the problem before these more drastic solutions were needed. Just below Tilbury Fort is the tiny Collier Signal Station perched on top of the sea wall. As colliers enter the river they receive their instructions from here as to which berth they are to make for, and how they are to proceed. The steam colliers revolutionized the coal traffic in many ways. Fewer ships were needed because they could each carry 600 tons of coal on average compared with the sailing collier's 200, they were faster, and they had a quicker turn-round because they could be ballasted for the return journey with water instead of gravel. By 1854 there were thirty-six steam colliers in service and by 1865 the vast coal traffic had passed almost entirely to steam.

One of the busiest coal wharves below Gravesend was in fact the basin of the Gravesend to Strood Canal. It had been decided in 1814, before the canal itself was finished, that the basin was outside the Port of London and it henceforth became a busy coal wharf supplying Gravesend and a wide district around. The canal had a curious history. It was the brainchild of the same indefatig-able Mr Ralph Dodd who had made the abortive attempt to

The Greenwich Royal Naval College
H.M.S. Worcester, *Greenhithe* (overleaf)

tunnel under the Thames between Tilbury and Gravesend. He in fact conceived both ideas at the same time, and in response to the same stimulus—the great invasion scare of 1778. Like the tunnel, the canal had primarily a military purpose—to provide a quick and safe means of carrying men and military material between the Thames and the Medway. The seven-mile-long canal would obviate the fifty-mile trip round the Hundred of Hoo, thus avoiding any risk of falling foul of French privateers which were very active in the estuary at this time. They frequently hung about the Nore and were a constant source of danger to the Navy's supply ships moving between London and the Medway ports. The canal would also reduce the dependence of sailing barges on tides and winds. Work started on the canal in 1801, but it was not opened until 1824, long after the Napoleonic Wars were over. Construction had been impeded by the great depth of the alluvial mud of the marshes; Mr Dodd, too, had forgotten to read the accounts of the building of Tilbury Fort. Because of these diffi- culties the original scheme to bring the canal out to the Thames at Higham Bight had been abandoned in favour of a route that kept closely to the edge of the marshes and met the River Thames near Gravesend. The other difficulty in the construction of the canal was the need to cross the hilly country of the Hundred of Hoo, and this was overcome by a tunnel $2\frac{1}{2}$ miles long. But the biggest snag of all arose in the actual operation of the canal when it was finished. Because of the big difference in water levels between the canal and the river, barges had to wait long periods in the Basin until tidal conditions were suitable for them to emerge. At times it would actually have been quicker to have sailed right round the long way, and cheaper as the canal dues would have been avoided. The canal was a dismal failure. It was therefore decided to run a railway through the tunnel to link Gravesend with Rochester, but to keep the canal open for navigation. The railway line was laid through the tunnel with one rail on the canal towpath and the other on trestles actually in the water. Thus both barges and trains used the same tunnel, a unique situation. Eventually the canal was filled in and a new double track line built through the tunnel by the South Eastern Railway. Probably few of the people travelling by train between Gravesend and Rochester realize that they are passing through an old canal tunnel. So the story of the Gravesend to Strood Canal

Gang of "muddies"—Lower
Medway, circa 1900
Shornmead Fort (preceding page)

The road to the Marshes—Cliffe
Cooling Castle

had a happy ending after all, and there are many yachtsmen who have reason to be grateful for Mr Dodd's expensive mistake since the old canal basin is now the headquarters of the Gravesend Sailing Club and is crowded with pleasure craft of all kinds.

Just beyond the canal basin at Denton is the newest addition to the Thameside scene—the £1 million National Sea Training School opened in May 1967, the largest and most modern of its kind in the world. Residential accommodation is provided for boys who are undergoing training before serving with the merchant navy. The facilities include a ship's bridge fully equipped with radar and other navigational aids, and the school has its own jetty on the Thames.

The forts of Tilbury and Gravesend were the keystones of a defensive arc which extended along both banks of the estuary. On the south bank Henry VIII had a blockhouse built at Higham Creek in 1553, the site appears as "Blockhouse Piece" on an old tithe map. During the Napoleonic Wars a fort was built at Shornmead about three miles below Gravesend, another at the Lower Hope and a third at East Tilbury. The latter was not the first on the site. As far back as 1402 the villagers of East Tilbury had been given permission to fortify their village after a French fleet had raided the Essex coast. Tradition says that the fort fired on De Ruyter's fleet in 1667 because the Dutch are said to have fired back and to have destroyed the church tower. There is certainly a plaque to that effect on the church, but somewhere I have heard a whisper that East Tilbury Church never had a tower! I much prefer the romantic version.

It is not easy for us at this remove in time to realize the intensity of the invasion fever that gripped this country during the early years of the French Revolution. In 1797 a new force called the "Sea Fencibles" was established, as a kind of coastal Home Guard, and in 1801 Nelson himself was appointed to defend the Thames Estuary. At about this time an order went out warning all people in the riverside areas to be ready to be moved at a moment's notice, and preparations were made for all the roads in these areas to be destroyed. Trinity House made arrangements for the river to be blocked in an emergency by the sinking of ships in the fairway. However, the scare passed over and eventually, with the return of peace, the fortifications were allowed to fall into disrepair. Some of them had been built hurriedly on the soft marsh, and like Henry VIII's blockhouse at Higham they soon subsided. By the mid-1860s, when the next invasion scare came long, many of them were completely useless. So it was that General Gordon found himself building the new Shornmead Fort, a much enlarged fort at Coalhouse Point, and entirely new forts at Cliffe, Slough near Allhallows, and on the Isle of Grain. The idea was that if any vessel survived the gunfire of these forts they would still have to pass through the jaws of the Tilbury–Gravesend pincer. In the film *General Gordon* the General is shown preparing the defences of Khartoum, with ingenious systems of cross-fire and makeshift land mines; it is intriguing to think that he was using experience he had gained in the Thames Estuary not so many years before. Happily these great forts were never seriously tested in war, although some of them were provided at intervals with modern equipment, including, in the case of Shornmead, torpedoes, and were manned during the 1939–45 War. Now, however, they are obsolete and mostly derelict. They are massively and solidly built so that they are unlikely to fall down as some of their predecessors did. They will remain, empty useless shells, plastered with warnings to members of the public and adventurous children not to venture past the padlocked doors —mute memorials to long forgotten anxieties.

On one occasion when I was collecting some local material in the village of Cliffe I met a very old inhabitant who gave me a much discoloured print of the old cement and whiting factory of Francis and Son which once occupied the huge chalk quarry in the area, together with extensive works at the nearby Cliffe Creek. The marsh is still littered with the ruins of this old factory, and the print shows the Creek crowded with shipping, steam-ships as well as sailing barges. Today the large new cement factory of the Alpha Cement Company carries on the centuries old tradition of chalk working at Cliffe. Instead of using Cliffe Creek this company takes its products by light railway across the marsh to a deep water jetty in Gravesend Reach where they are loaded into ocean–going ships.

Cliffe has an abundance of that other essential ingredient for cement-making—clay. At first it was thought that only river mud was suitable for cement-making and the marsh clays from the reclaimed land behind the sea wall were never used. An extensive industry grew up along the Thames and Medway wherever there were any saltings suitable for excavation. The most extensive area worked was the Stoke Saltings of the Lower Medway, but the saltings of Higham Bight were also extensively worked, with permanent effects on the configuration of the coastline. Later, as new processes of cement manufacture came into use it was found that marsh clay could be used quite satisfactorily. The cement companies then began a rush to buy up as much marsh clay land as they were likely to need. Large areas of the Cliffe levels were acquired in this way before the war, and excavation has been going on now for many years. The result has been a transformation of the landscape of the whole area. Hundreds of acres of flooded marsh comprise almost an inland sea, with quite sizeable waves being generated when the wind blows across the flat marshes. To reduce the erosion cross walls of clay have been left which divide the excavations into a succession of huge basins. There was once a scheme for a seaplane base at Cliffe . . . as it is now I think seaplanes could land there already! It is an irony of history that part of this land was reclaimed from the river at great cost by Lord Darnley in 1815. The possibility of refilling the flooded pits is one which has exercised the planners for many years; one possibility is that dredgings from the river might be deposited in them. What a curious stratification for some future geologist that would be!

From the village of Cliffe a road dips steeply down to the level of the marshes, past the "No Through Road" sign, and then wanders aimlessly across them until it peters out at Lower Hope Point. A battery had been erected at this strategic spot during the Napoleonic scare, but it had survived only a few years. The only fighting it ever witnessed was the illegal bare fist fighting of the nineteenth century; the pugilists would come down by boat knowing that they would be reasonably safe in this remote spot. In 1901 the site was swallowed up in a great explosives factory which occupied a mile of river frontage, with two jetties and a wharf. By the time the 1914–18 War broke out this Curtiss and Harvey factory had become, to quote a contemporary description: "The largest and most completely equipped explosives factory in the kingdom". It had some 2,000 men working on the site, and the road from Cliffe village was made up at this time. Many trees were planted on the otherwise treeless marshes to reduce the effect of any explosions. With the end of the war, and the subsequent rationalization of Britain's explosives industry, under the Nobel Group, the Thameside industry came to an end. It had always been a "finishing" industry, and was too far from the source of the raw material to survive the rationalization process. By 1922 this great industry had become a ghost of the past . . . and ghostly indeed is the effect produced when the wind whistles through the ruins, and the trees, of the Lower Hope, the sense of utter isolation magnified by the tolling of the marker buoy out in the river.

Cliffe village is an old and historic place with an air of past glories. One local resident I once met in Cliffe invited me into her home to see the fine collection she had made of Roman pottery found on the marshes only a stone's throw away. There was so much of it that the site must obviously have been a Romano-British pottery. Sitting on top of its imposing cliff, and dominating the Lower Hope as it does, Cliffe was clearly a place of some importance in the past. It may even have been the site of the Synod of Clovesho in 803, although there are several other claimants. The village has a fine church and a wide buttway outside where the people once practised with their long bows. The rectors of Cliffe have had special privileges rarely possessed by the incumbents of country parishes (although this apparently did not include the privilege of making their sermons too long as there is a large hour glass on the pulpit). Curious as this may seem today Cliffe was a port of some consequence in 1326 and was used by vessels of up to fifty tons. This was of course before the marshes were reclaimed. One Cliffe farmer told me that the remains of an old boat had been dug up from the marsh clay at his farm—a common enough occurrence, you may say, in riverside districts . . . but the name of the farm is Wharf Farm which certainly suggests that the river came up here at one time. Today it is a mile or so away. Cliffe seems to have declined steadily from the fourteenth century onwards, until Hasted was able to write of the place in 1797: "Cliffe seems daily growing into further ruin and poverty, the number of inhabitants lessening yearly and several of the houses, for want of them, lying in ruins." The cause of the town's decline was almost certainly the ague that followed the enclosure of the marshes. I once examined the parish records of the burials at Cliffe for the year 1876, and I found that of twenty-three burials, only four were over 55, the others were mainly babies or children. The location of the cement factory here in the 1860s, and the improved drainage leading to the diminution and eventual disappearance of the ague, marked the beginning of Cliffe's awakening from its long sleep. However, old attitudes die hard. One old resident of the town said to me, "Cliffe is dead in more sense than one—the cement gets into their hearts and hardens them." Let me hasten to say that I have never found this to be so, I have always been well received on my visits there. Of course modern methods of transport have done much to break down old isolations, although the railway through the Hundred of Hoo was not very effective in this regard since the station was a mile away from the village. The line was heading for the new port of embarkation for the Continent at Port Victoria on the Isle of Grain, and the builders paid little heed to the needs of the villagers of the Hundred. In recent years Cliffe has been one of the places suggested as a suitable location for London's third airport. The people of Cliffe do not take this too seriously. They remind you that the Lower Hope was always the most notorious reach in the river for fogs. Did not Arthur Young during his tour of Essex in 1807 speak of the "thick and stinking fogs"? And did not the convict escape from the prison hulk in dense fog in *Great Expectations*? Charles Dickens lived at Gadshill; he knew his estuary.

Even today the people of the marshland villages on both banks have very little contact with each other across the water. Ask a group of people in Cliffe where the villages of Mucking, Fobbing, Corringham or Vange are and most of them will not know. But it was not always so. Before the marshes were enclosed the river highway linked together a hundred Wharf Farms more effectively than any roads could do before the internal combustion engine. Someone has remarked upon the way in which the movements of the two rebel forces advancing on London along their respective banks during Jack Straw's Rebellion 1381 were so well co-ordinated. Indeed the rebellion broke out among the Thameside fishermen and no doubt they had more than grievances in common. One important link in the cross-river communications of this period was the ancient causeway and ferry at Higham. Very little is known about this, but without doubt it was the main pilgrim route to Canterbury for the whole of this part of Essex. Tilbury was avoided because of the width of the marshes there, although the proximity of Gravesend would otherwise have made this the obvious site for a crossing. The long spur to East Tilbury offered better access to the river on the north bank, and the ferry in fact went across the river from Coalhouse Point to Higham Causeway, passing the Sun Inn at Higham, which used to be called the "Old Ferry House", and the site of an ancient nunnery which moved here in 1280 to serve the pilgrims and to profit from their charity. At the time of Domesday the parishes of Gravesend, Higham and Chalk all possessed land on the Essex shore, as was the case at Woolwich. The old thirty-feet-wide causeway across the marshes at Higham can still be seen. Some insight into the usefulness of the ferry is gained from an entry in the records of the Wardens of Rochester Bridge. During the Fifteenth Century the ferry was owned by the Manor of Southall, which was one of the manors on the Essex shore contributing to the upkeep of the bridge at Rochester. In 1449–50, according to these old records: "100s. was allowed to Thomas Castell, farmer of East Tilbury, because the ferry there was not occupied this year in the summer by reason of the disturbance of the commonalty [apparently a reference to the activities of the private armies roaming about just before the out-break of the Wars of the Roses], and it is testified that the ferry is an excellent source of profit to the said manor." When the blockhouse was built at Tilbury by Henry VII this necessitated the building of a road across the marshes to the fort and after that the Higham Ferry ceased to operate in favour of the new "short ferry" to Gravesend.

The northern land-fall of the Higham Ferry, the long straggling village of East Tilbury, is one of the most remote and quietest villages of the Estuary. It is literally, as its name implies, "at the end of the road". As so often happens with the villages of the estuary the road through the village leads down to the marshes, where there is a riverside battery, and then just peters out at the sea wall. Defoe, after describing Tilbury Fort, continued: "From here there is nothing for many miles together remarkable but a continued level of unhealthy marshes." The marshes are no longer unhealthy, but otherwise his comment, except in one particular, remains basically true today for the north bank of the Lower Hope. There is a remarkable continuity of family history in these river-side villages. Some years ago, whilst in East Tilbury, I met an elderly gentleman whose name was Mott. The name was familiar, and going back to the notes I had made after a study of the old records of the Commissioners of Sewers for the East Tilbury area I found frequent references to the Mott family from 1690 to the present day—this in a village of 300 people. On revisiting East Tilbury only a short time ago, however, I was struck by the number of new houses which have been erected there in the last few years. It is fast losing its old-world atmosphere. Which brings me to the one particular in which Defoe's comment no longer holds. If Defoe were alive today nothing would astonish him more than the great Bata Shoe Factory and workers' estate just north of East Tilbury. He was an industrialist himself—at any rate he managed to lose quite a lot of money on a tile factory somewhere near East Tilbury. But never in his wildest entrepreneurial dreams could he have visualized such a factory as this. I do not know of any other factory of this size in Britain that has a more rural location. As there are no towns of any size to speak of nearby Batas simply had to build homes for the workers alongside the factory. And not only homes but a large hotel, swimming pool, tennis courts, cinema and extensive sports fields, everything in fact that a town should have except diversity of occupation. Everyone's neighbour makes shoes. But this may be a small price to pay for a job out in the country, with a view of the River Thames from every factory window, at any rate a good number of the 3,000 workers at the factory seem to think so. What vision it must have needed in 1932–3 to have chosen this of all sites: after he had got over his initial surprise I think Defoe might have approved.

Defoe's contemptuous dismissal of East Tilbury would also embrace its neighbour Mucking. Mucking is a village, or what remains of a village, which has an environment as unattractive as its name, which, by the way, the inhabitants once tried to have altered but unsuccessfully. Once a fishing port of considerable importance, Mucking is now sandwiched between the huge refuse disposal dump occupying a large part of the foreshore to the east and south, extensive old gravel workings to the north, and the railway to the west. It has shrunk to an insignificant appendage of its larger neighbour Stanford le Hope. The church is remarkable only for the inscription on the tomb of one Elizabeth Downes who died in 1667; it reads: "She lived happily with four husbands." We are not told whether she achieved this feat contemporaneously or not!

Our explorations round the villages of the Lower Hope and Gravesend Reach have brought us to the doorstep of the great oil refineries of the estuary at Thameshaven and Shellhaven. But before we take this step from the rural seclusion of the Thameside villages to the futuristic world of gasoline and methane, and all their associated "ines" and "anes", we must retrace our steps to the south bank; for we have not yet explored the fascinating and beautiful country of the Hundred of Hoo.

15

THE HUNDRED OF HOO

The strange elbow of land that lies between the Thames and the Medway is called the Hundred of Hoo. It is a curiously isolated and remote corner of Kent, more remote than any other part of the Home Counties—and less visited. Which is a pity, because it has a strong earthy appeal of its own, the appeal of wide open rolling countryside with few hedges, of wide open skies, of wide open views of marsh and river. And not least, it is as historic a region as its name suggests, with many tiny villages which, although not exactly pretty in the picture-book sense, yet have a quiet air of genuine rurality about them very far removed from the artificiality of so many commuter villages the same distance from London.

Geologically speaking, the Hundred of Hoo is a long whale-back of London Clay which meets the River Thames at All-hallows, and has a small outlier in the Isle of Grain, cut off from the Hundred by the Yantlet Channel. All round the long coast of the Hundred, about forty miles, are the marshes, sometimes $2\frac{1}{2}$ miles wide. The present coast line, represented by the earthen river wall, is in fact entirely an artificial one. It is the result of piecemeal enclosure over the centuries. The now obsolete river walls of previous enclosures are called "old Counter walls" on the detailed maps; they are used by the farmers for ready access to their sheep flocks on the marshes (these marshes on the south bank, for some unknown reason, have never been ploughed), and also act as a reserve line of defence if the main wall should be breached. The marsh farmers have some hair-raising stories to tell of what happens when the walls are over-topped, or breached, by extraordinary high tides. The water rushes across the flat marshes faster than a man can run. Fortunately this very rarely happens, and with modern systems of advance warning of very high tides no farmer should become trapped by floods. Walking along the river wall, without seeing a soul for hours on end, and miles away from any sign of human habitation, with the river on one side, and a green sea of grass on the other (often at a much lower level), is an exhilarating experience. Beyond the river wall are the so-called Blyth Sands, most inappropriately named as they seem to be nothing but a vast expanse of mud. It is the existence of this natural barrier that has so far prevented the Hundred of Hoo from being developed for industrial use. However, there is access to deep water at the Lower Hope (where the explosives factory used to be) and it may not be many years before industries needing plenty of space, and remoteness from heavily populated areas, come to this area. It is probably the last substantial area in the Estuary suitable for industrial development which has not yet been exploited. I rather hope it remains that way. I have seen a reference somewhere to the fact, if it is a fact, that during the invasion scare of 1801–3 the French planned to land an army along this stretch of shore—like the Allies in the last war, landing on the Normandy shore, the French would thus have chosen the least likely location.

Overlooking the marshes, and a very lonely windswept spot it is, lies the hamlet of Cooling. The place is notable for two reasons. First, in the graveyard of the church can be seen the last resting place of the Comport family. Here may still be seen the little lozenge-shaped graves that Charles Dickens describes so exactly in the opening paragraphs of *Great Expectations*: ". . . five little stone lozenges each about a foot and a half long". There can be no doubt that Dickens had these graves in mind; he was often seen striding around the marshland villages. What he may not have realized is that the thirteen children of the Comport family who died so close together at the end of the eighteenth century, were almost certainly victims of the ague, and in particular of the macabre habit of the Anopheles mosquito of remaining most of its life under the roof of the houses where it obtains its first meals of blood. The Comports were about the last wealthy family to stay in the Hundred and they paid a heavy price for their "loyalty"—theirs was almost certainly one of the notorious "malarious houses" of the Hundred. One has some sympathy for the author of the *Steamboat Companion* of 1823, one of the new guides written to amuse the growing number of people who travelled down the river on the new steamboats: "Who would believe that for six months in the year the shores of the Hundred of Hoo were only to be explored by the amphibious, that the sun is seldom seen for the fog, and that every creature in love with life flees the swamps of Hoo, preferring any station to its ague-dealing vapours, its fenny filth and its muddy flats?" Good journalistic stuff . . . but there was more than a grain of truth in it before the middle of the nineteenth century.

The other notable feature of Cooling is its great castle, built in 1382 soon after the sacking of Gravesend by the French. That must indeed have been a traumatic experience judging by the impact it had on the development of the whole region. However, one must not jump to conclusions. It is just possible that the French invasion was a convenient excuse for the Brookes to build a castle for the better protection of their own property against an unruly populace rather than as protection from the French. The peasants who revolted in 1381 could not however be accused of being unpatriotic. They ordered all those who came from areas within twelve miles of the coast to return to their homes for fear of a French invasion. The castle was built only a year after the Peasants' Revolt which broke out in North Kent. It is a huge structure surrounded by a massive wall and a wide moat, now dry. Although it is now 2½ miles from the river, there is no doubt that when it was built the Thames waters washed its walls and filled its moat. In 1847 confirmation of this was received when the remains of a large vessel were unearthed during work on the walls. The castle suffered considerable damage during the Wyatt Rebellion of 1554 when it was defended by Lord Cobham, some say as a blind to enable him to join the rebels with whom he was thought to have many sympathies. Today the old castle is more or less in ruins (the walls were built of solid chalk faced with flints, unlike Hadleigh Castle across the water which was built with Kentish Ragstone floated down the Medway) but there is a private residence within the walls and the whole place has a great sense of quiet and peace.

The ghost town of Allhallows-on-Sea is a great contrast to the rest of the villages of the Hundred, or indeed to the village of Allhallows only half a mile away. It is a product of the twentieth century that somehow went wrong. In the early 1920s the short stretch of river frontage at Bell's Hard, near Allhallows village, became so popular as a rendezvous for motorists out for an afternoon drive that the local farmers decided to make an honest penny (at a time when it was not too easy to make one in farming) by providing car parks, toilets and a refreshment booth. The numbers using the facilities steadily increased, and it was not long before a company was formed to develop the potential of the site more seriously. They even proposed to call the new resort "Thamesmouth", but they eventually settled for the more modest "on-Sea" instead. That involves rather a stretch of the imagination, especially when the tide goes out, but presumably they thought if Leigh and Southend could get away with it so could they. At this point in the story, about 1932, the railway company decided to build a short branch line to Allhallows-on-Sea from the Hundred of Hoo line. Its success was immediate. Thousands of Londoners took advantage of the cheap excursion tickets offered and swarmed down to this new seaside resort, far nearer to South and South-east London than any other seaside resort. It was only a matter of time before someone had the idea of taking the whole thing even further. And how far they wanted to go! There were schemes for zoological gardens, a physical training stadium, the largest swimming pool in the country complete with artificial waves, and a holiday camp and amusement park four times the size of Blackpool's. However, all these schemes came to naught except a part of the amusement park. The war came along and all work was stopped. The scenic railway was dismantled to give a clear field of fire for Slough Fort, another of the chain of forts built by General Gordon. Allhallows-on-Sea became a ghost town at the end of the railway. After the war there was a scheme in 1956 to build a new town here of 25,000 people to house the workers of the giant new oil refinery being built on the Isle of Grain, but it fell through after objections on agricultural grounds. So Allhallows-on-Sea remained undeveloped. When I revisited it a short time ago I was surprised to see that the whole of the riverside has been laid out as a permanent caravan site, and holiday flatlets, by the Strood Rural District Council. It has all been tastefully done, but seen from the northern bank Allhallows-on-Sea still presents a rather ugly blemish in the otherwise totally rural front which the Hundred presents to the Thames.

And so we come to the historic Yantlet Creek which divides the Isle of Grain from the Hundred of Hoo. The Isle of Grain is strictly speaking not in the Hundred at all. It was associated in past centuries with Minister in Sheppey, and this naturally makes one wonder whether at one time the Medway entered the Thames via the Yantlet Channel, an idea which receives some support from the old tradition that there was once a ford linking the Isle of Grain to Sheppey. But all this is conjecture—so far as recorded history goes the Isle of Grain has always been an island cut off by the Medway from the Isle of Sheppey, and by the Yantlet from the Hundred of Hoo. The Yantlet Channel was the traditional route for all smaller coasting vessels for many centuries. In those days there was a stone bridge linking Grain to the Hundred with a high central arch high enough for vessels with stepped masts to pass underneath. Even today the causeway is still called "Grain Bridge". However, in time the channel became silted up and navigation virtually ceased, the bridge apparently collapsed and was replaced by a causeway. On Thursday, September 18th 1833 occurred one of the most curious incidents in the history of the Island. Mr Ralph Arnold has told the story in more detail in his excellent book *The Hundred of Hoo*. Gangs of workmen employed by the Corporation of London suddenly descended on the causeway and started to excavate a channel six feet deep and twenty-five feet wide across it. The Corporation explained to the astonished islanders, who were being cut off from the mainland, that as Conservators of the Thames and Lower Medway they had decided to reopen Yantlet Channel to afford a safer passage for small vessels than the journey round the Nore, and to improve the supply of fish to the capital. However, the farmers and landowners of Grain rose up in protest and the case was taken to the High Court. In addition to the main argument that for a very long time the creek had been closed to navigation and no protest had been made, the villagers pointed out that the smugglers who frequented the area would be better able to frustrate the coastguards stationed at the northern entrance to the creek. Eventually the City lost the case and the causeway was restored. It was a strange attempt to put the clock back possibly hundreds of years, and one of the underlying purposes of the Corporation may have been their desire to establish that they had jurisdiction, as Conservators, over the Lower Medway as well as the Thames. If so they lost this battle since the High Court decided that the City's jurisdiction extended only to the mouth of the Yantlet.

Today, with the huge refinery located on the adjacent marshes, it is difficult to realize how isolated from civilization the Isle of Grain once was. It was one of the most notorious places for ague in the whole estuary and as late as 1876 three-quarters of the people of the village suffered from the disease. Few people visited the village, and those living there had few contacts with the outside world. In 1904 there was a man living there who had never been away from the island for a week at a time in his whole life, and he was 83. Said the *Sheerness Guardian* in 1905: "For hundreds of years the small hamlet has slumbered (it can hardly be said to nestle) peacefully along to the measured beat of life." The Isle of Grain was typical of the other villages in this backwater of North Kent. At nearby St Mary's Hoo, for instance, there was a rector who had never delivered a single sermon in his fifty-nine years' ministry. He always insisted that the men should sit on one side of the church and women and children on the other. The population of this village increased by only four over the whole of the nineteenth century. However, the peacefulness of the Isle of Grain in 1905 was not what it had been even then. In 1866, for instance, General Gordon had built one of the largest of his forts on this strategic island commanding the Medway Estuary. It is still there down by the shore and the inevitable line of coastguard cottages—a huge grey vault of a building, cold and dead; but once there were a thousand men stationed here. Then there was the arrival of the South Eastern railway in 1883 to serve the newly constructed timber jetty at the grandiosely named Port Victoria. The name was not only a compliment to the reigning sovereign, but was intended as a riposte to their bitter rivals the London, Chatham and Dover Railway who had only a few years pre-viously opened a railhead at Queenborough across the Medway. The two lines were competing for cross-channel passenger traffic. The Port Victoria route proved quite popular with royalty, to whom its greatest asset was its extreme isolation from cheering crowds, but it was not much patronized by the general public and was soon discontinued. There is some evidence that the ulterior object behind the Port Victoria development was that it might become an out-port for London, but the building of the Tilbury Docks, and the growth of Thameshaven, killed these schemes. But if the peacefulness of the Isle of Grain in 1905 had been already disturbed this was as nothing to what was to come in the

1950s when the Anglo-Iranian Oil Company, as it was then, decided to build their great refinery there. This we must leave for the next chapter, but it shattered in one blow any pretensions to rural peacefulness that the Isle of Grain may still have had left to it.

A very much older industry (if it can be called an industry— it certainly provided employment to a lot of people) in the Isle of Grain was smuggling. Nearly everyone was engaged in it in some form or other, from the parson to the shepherd, even if it merely took the form of a conspiracy of silence. Nearly every hard or landing place round the coastline of the Hundred was used for the landing of contraband and every village, almost every old house, has its own crop of smugglers' tales. A tunnel seems to be connected with every smugglers' tale. Take Allhallows, for instance. There is supposed to be a smugglers' tunnel under the road between the church (contraband was often stored in the churches) and the cottages opposite. When the workmen were digging the Gravesend to Strood canal in the 1820s they came across a tunnel running across the marshes from the old mill on the riverside at Denton to Gravesend. No doubt the mill had been erected partially as a blind, just as many houses were refaced during the nineteenth century as a cover to the building of caches and tunnels inside. When Colonel Loftus, the noted Essex historian invited me to join him some years ago on an expedition to search for dene holes near his home at Low Street, East Tilbury, we not only came across what was almost certainly a collapsed dene hole but we found also the entrance to a tunnel in the side of a pit near East Tilbury Church. Yantlet Creek was very popular with the smugglers because of its remoteness. They used Gantlebor Island, a mud flat off the mouth of the Creek, as their depot and operated from there along both banks of the estuary until eventually a coastguard watch vessel of 167 tons was stationed there. In the 1890s she was replaced by a coastguard watch house by the mouth of the Creek, and a lonely spot it is too.

Before the Preventive Water Guard (later the Coastguard Service) was established in 1831 patrols of dragoons were stationed round the coast to deal with smugglers. These were then replaced by officers and men of the new force who were stationed in old hulks anchored at such lonely backwaters as Cliffe Creek, Colemouth Creek, Holehaven and Tilbury. These hulks are not to be confused (although the way of life may not have seemed much different to the men stationed there!) with the convict hulks which were also anchored at lonely spots in the estuary. Here prisoners were accommodated whilst awaiting transportation to the Antipodes. The fishermen of the estuary still refer to Sea Reach where some of the hulks were stationed as "Botany".

There are some excellent viewpoints in the Hundred of Hoo, but none to compare with the views to be obtained near All-hallows. Just westwards of the church is a spot where one can look both ways, across the estuary of the Thames to the north, and southwards across the Lower Medway. I know of no finer viewpoint in the Home Counties. The view southwards is completely different today from what it was a hundred years ago, quite apart from the oil refinery, and the huge new power station being built at Kingsnorth. It was about a hundred years ago that the extensive area of the Stoke Saltings (saltings are marshes which are not protected from the river and are therefore covered by every tide) began to be worked for the mud required by the new and rapidly expanding cement industry. Barge owners would contract with the cement companies for the supply of mud and they would then acquire a piece of saltings from which they proceeded to strip the top ten or fifteen feet of mud, loading it into barges to be taken round to the Thameside cement factories. When the mud had been stripped they moved on to another piece of the Salting.

For forty years, between 1860 and 1900, this curious industry was carried on entirely by hand labour, and about a hundred "muddies", or "mud-slingers" as they were also called, were employed. They came from the local villages and earned wages up to £5 per week which was good money for those days. They were strong muscular men and apparently enjoyed good health while they remained on the job, although many died of heart trouble after they retired. Some of the men spent their wages as quickly as they earned them, and the local public houses were never short of custom. But others saved their money and moved to the other side of the bar; it was said in the Hundred that the ex-muddies cornered the public-house business! Some years ago, being anxious to find a picture of the muddies in action, and having heard about their ownership of public houses, I went to one of the public houses in the area and asked the proprietor, who turned out to have been an ex-muddie, if he could find me a picture. At first he said he did not have any, but suddenly he remembered that an old photograph was being used as a backing for another picture in a frame on the wall. We took the picture down and there was the old photograph. Naturally it was extremely rare for photographs to be taken when the working face was often a mile from the shore along a slippery marshy track totally submerged at high tide.

As soon as the barge had floated into its position on the salting the gang of men allotted to that ship swould start loading the mud into it. They had to load 150 tons in the six hours or so of the ebb tide. With the next flood tide the boat would be lifted off the mud and would then sail round the Nore to the cement factories. The men were equipped with a kind of spade called a "fly tool", made of wood with a long narrow blade fitted with a steel plate to make the clay "fly" off. The men worked on ledges one foot wide. The man working on the upper ledge had to throw further, but the man on the lower and nearer ledge had higher to throw. They stripped for the work and sweated profusely. The wear on their hands was so great that they developed hard skin and could not clench their fists. They wore special leather boots with canvas leggings, and worked through the night with the aid of "blizzy lamps", a kind of hurricane lamp. Now only the memories remain—and even these are rapidly disappearing as there must be few people alive today who participated in this curious industry. Yet when the last survivor has died there will still remain the permanent memorial to their activities in the landscape of the Stoke Saltings. Where at one time thousands of sheep used to graze, there is now only a vast morass of mud with hundreds of islands of unworked clay (called the "Callow" by the muddies) and long thin fingers of land stretching out from the mainland which were the access routes to the working faces. Few local industries of this size can ever have had such a devastating effect on the landscape.

16

FROM WOODEN SCHOONER TO
SUPER TANKER

Oil and petrol play so large a part in our lives today that it comes as something of a shock to realize that petroleum was only discovered as recently as 1859, and has been in commercial use for only about a hundred years. The first cargo of petroleum arrived in London in 1861, not in tanks, or even oil drums, but in wooden barrels! And it was no super tanker that brought it but a wooden sailing brig of 224 tons, the *Elizabeth Watts*. Naturally the barrels suffered damage during the rough crossings and the ships arrived in the Thames full of petroleum fumes so that there were several serious explosions. As we saw earlier, these led to the passing of the Petroleum Act of 1871 which prohibited any vessel laden with a cargo of petroleum from proceeding: ". . . above or westward of Thameshaven". So it was that, sheltered by this Act, the Thames Estuary became the location for the early petroleum installations, and eventually the largest oil refining centre in Britain and one of the largest in Europe.

The choice of Thameshaven was no accident. It was an obvious place for such a limit since it had deep water, the wide Sea Reach with safe anchorage and room to manœuvre, an existing railhead to London, and perhaps the greatest asset of all at the time—space and remoteness from residential districts. These natural advantages had not passed unnoticed before this. As far back as 1815 a group of Billingsgate fish merchants, irritated by the delays experienced by shipping in the upper river, which often caused fish to be jettisoned, conceived the novel idea of a "rail road" from Holehaven to London. However, they did not receive enough support for the project and it languished for another twenty years. Then in 1840 a company was established to build a new out-port for London at the newly-designated "Thameshaven".

It was planned to deal with London's requirements of fish, coal and other cargoes, and it would also handle an expected million passengers every year. An enthusiastic contemporary journalist wrote: "Thameshaven in a few years may become a second Liverpool where dock land is worth a guinea an inch." But all these brave hopes came to nothing. It was indeed another fifteen years before Thameshaven was built at all, and then it was merely as a jetty for the landing of live cattle. Like Tilbury, Thameshaven was years before its time. Landings of live cattle were slow at first but after the great Cattle Plague of 1865, which was followed by severe regulations prohibiting the landing of live cattle except at certain wharves, of which Thameshaven was one, they increased more rapidly. Between the years 1868 and 1876 about one-third of all the live cattle imported into Britain entered through Thameshaven. However, the Law gave, and the Law took away. In 1876 following a serious outbreak of foot and mouth disease an order was passed prohibiting the import of live cattle from most continental countries except for immediate slaughter. Thameshaven was not equipped for slaughter and the order in effect gave a virtual monopoly to the newly established Deptford Foreign Cattle Market. Thence onwards only a trickle of live cattle passed through Thameshaven until 1894 when the development of refrigeration virtually put an end to the import of live cattle from overseas.

It was fortunate for the proprietors of Thameshaven that as one industry collapsed another was born. In 1876, the year of the collapse of the cattle trade, a small petroleum storage installation was located at Thameshaven, at first for the storage of oil in barrels and then after 1880 for bulk storage. Up to 1914 almost every gallon of oil that was imported into London entered through Thameshaven. Still, the company concerned, the London and Thameshaven Oil Wharves Limited, continued to expand until by 1923 it claimed to have the largest storage capacity in the world for the public storage of oil. In 1916 the monopoly of the London and Thameshaven Oil Wharves Limited came to an end with the establishment at Shellhaven, alongside Thameshaven, of an oil refinery by the Anglo Saxon Petroleum Company, later incorporated into the Shell Group. The coincidence of the two names has led to the suggestion that they are linked in some way, but that is not so. The name Shellhaven is shown on a map of the time of Henry VIII, and the oil company took its name from the fact that its founder traded in ornamental shells from the East. Other refineries soon followed, although none of them on a large scale. In 1921 the London and Thameshaven Oil Wharves themselves erected a refinery, and in the same year Cory Brothers, the national coal factors, turned to the manufacture and distribution of oil products. They built a refinery on the 1,500-acre estate previously owned by Kynoch and Company, the explosives manufacturers, and renamed the little community on the marshes Coryton—its previous name was Kynochtown.

It is worth digressing a moment to recall the meteoric rise and fall of the great Kynoch explosives factory, which parallels in many ways that of Curtiss and Harvey's across the water. Kynochs acquired land on the marshes near Thameshaven in 1897 and two years later they had built a large factory for the manufacture of explosives. The factory was linked to the village of Corringham on the "mainland", $2\frac{1}{2}$ miles distant across the marshes, by a light railway. The company also built a small village for key workers adjacent to the works and called it Kynochtown. A dreary isolated place it was, hemmed in between the oil tanks and the explosives factory and miles from civilization; it was so isolated that the village hall was licensed both for the solemnization of marriage and the sale of intoxicating liquor! About 500 workers were employed at the factory in those pre-1914 days, most of them living in ugly red brick houses built in the ancient village of Corringham, and travelling to and fro in the light railway. Then came the Great War and the numbers of workers rapidly increased so that the staggering daily total of 10,000 passenger journeys on the little light railway was recorded. The train of fourteen coaches, pulled by two locomotives, solemnly pulled out of Coryton's miniscule station, chugged the $2\frac{1}{2}$ miles across the marshes, disgorged its passengers at Corringham and returned for more. After the war the factory closed down and the oil industry, which replaced it, did not employ so many workers, so the number of workers using the railway declined. However, it remained open until 1951. It was the only standard gauge railway in Britain with a passenger service entirely isolated from any other passenger train service.

To return to our main theme. There were three relatively minor developments in the oil industry during the inter-war years. A small storage works was erected at the western end of Canvey

Island, near Holehaven, in 1938, and small refineries were erected at the Isle of Grain (1923) and at Kingsnorth a little further up the Medway (1930s). None of these was large but they were significant, in retrospect, as setting the stage for the enormous development that was to come after the 1939–45 War.

A major change in policy after the war, as regards the location of oil refineries, was responsible for the huge investments in the Thames Estuary that transformed its landscape and its whole economy. Whereas before the war the refineries had generally been located as near as possible to the producing areas, now it was decided to import the crude oil and refine it in Britain as far as possible. The Thames Estuary was an obvious candidate for a substantial share of this expansion, and during the 1950s three massive developments took place; at Shellhaven (Shell Oil Company), at Coryton (Mobil Oil Company) and at the Isle of Grain (British Petroleum Oil Company). In addition a new refinery is now being built by United Refineries on Canvey Island. As a result of these developments the Port of London accounts for just over two-thirds of the total value of oil imported into the United Kingdom, more than any other oil refining centre in this country. With a refining capacity of 23.2 million metric tons, the Thames Estuary is now the third largest oil refining centre in Europe, after the Rotterdam area (32.25 million) and the River Seine (24.6 million).

One of the main engineering problems which had to be overcome at each of these new refineries was that of providing the millions of gallons of water required. Obviously the water had to be taken from the Thames and Medway, but the problem was How? Different solutions were adopted. At Shellhaven a shaft was sunk in the bed of the river opposite the refinery and connected by an underground tunnel to a sunken pump house on the marshes; at Coryton a huge 4,200 tons concrete caisson was floated down-river from Gravesend, where it had been made, and placed on a prepared platform on the river bed where it was used to house the pumps to draw water direct from the river. At the Isle of Grain the problem was especially difficult because the volume of water flowing down the Medway is less than in the Thames, and this necessitated the building of a reservoir on the foreshore of the refinery which is filled at high tide and then used to maintain the flow during low tide.

Engineering problems are not the only ones; there are sociologi-cal problems as well. New refineries represent large new centres of employment, and hence the pressure to establish new towns to accommodate the influx of workers and their families reasonably near their jobs. We saw in the last chapter how the scheme for a "refinery town" at Allhallows-on-Sea foundered, the workers now having to travel out from neighbouring towns by bus and car. But on the north bank there is no large centre of population reasonably near at hand, and therefore a new town has been created around the existing marsh-edge villages of Stanford le Hope, Corringham and Fobbing. Corringham New Town is the smallest, and without doubt the least known, of all London's post-war new towns. It suffers in this respect from its close proxi-mity to the much larger new town of Basildon. The main coastal road to Southend skirts Corringham New Town and Stanford le Hope, but probably few of those who hurtle along this long straight stretch of road realize that the block of new buildings occupying the crest of the hills to the east are in fact the centre of Corringham New Town. It is an attractive town, but I was a little disappointed to find that nowhere is there a view of the River Thames—the town faces northwards, whilst its whole *raison d'être* is the river.

On Canvey Island there has been a conflict of interest ever since the first rumours of an oil industry in the 1920s. There was much antagonism when the 1938 development took place, and again in 1964 when plans were announced for the new refinery to be built near South Benfleet on the eastern side of the island and on the opposite side from the present oil installations. Some 17,000 objectors in the area signed a petition of protest. The people of South Benfleet, occupying the high country immediately over-looking the marshes on which the refinery is to be built, were particularly concerned at the possibility of offensive fumes. How-ever, the scheme was eventually approved and the contractors are now on the site. The plain fact is that the number of suitable sites in the estuary is now limited and the last remaining ones are at a high premium. Nevertheless it does seem rather strange that the open marshland on the south bank, far away from inhabited areas, remains undeveloped, whilst Canvey Island, with about 20,000 inhabitants and many thousands of holiday-makers, has to have a refinery built on its back doorstep. Presumably the problem of the Blyth Sands could be met by piping the oil from deepwater anchorages. On the other hand there is no denying that the rateable value of a new refinery, perhaps equal to that represented by several thousand houses, can enable the people of Canvey Island to improve their public services more quickly than would otherwise be possible. These are indeed difficult questions to weigh in the balance; maybe we shall all be using natural gas one day (as the inhabitants of Canvey Island, by one of those twists of irony, already are) and the problems of where to site oil refineries will be forgotten.

A great question mark hangs over the future of the oil industry in the Thames Estuary. Can it meet the changing requirements of the great super-tankers now coming into service, and the even bigger ones being planned? The situation at present is that tankers of up to 100,000 tons can reach Thameshaven fully laden. In March 1967 the tanker *World Friendship*, 90,000 tons deadweight, steamed up to Thameshaven. She is 870 feet long and required 45 feet of water. Even with the help of the tide, there was only five feet to spare under the keel. The nervous strain on the pilot of bringing such a huge vessel up the river, with so small a margin, can well be imagined. But already vessels of 100,000 tons (bigger than the *Queen Mary*) are small by present day standards for oil tankers. Ships of 200,000 tons are already in service (they have oil tanks as big as St Paul's Cathedral), whilst the Gulf Oil Company has announced plans for super-tankers of 300,000 tons to use Bantry Bay in Southern Ireland as a distributing centre for Western Europe. Plans for tankers of 500,000 tons are already taking shape in Japan, and the experts say that there is no technical reason why tankers of up to one millions tons should not be built. Can the Thames Estuary stay in the race? The depth of water is inadequate for tankers of over 100,000 tons fully laden, but there is no reason why tankers of 200,000 tons could not berth in the river if they are only partially laden, i.e. if they have unloaded part of their oil elsewhere, say at Rotterdam. The oil companies of Thameside are now making plans to receive such tankers. They are also experimenting with techniques of mooring tankers in mid-stream, where the water is deepest, and pumping the oil ashore by pipeline. The mooring point would be so designed as to allow the tanker to move through an arc of 360 degrees according to the state of wind or tide. But so far as ships of around

The Creek—Queenborough

500,000 tons are concerned, the Thames Estuary falls out of the picture—the water simply is not deep enough. Where will the process end? We may see a few million-ton tankers commuting between the oil fields and a few fixed distributing centres blessed by Nature with very deep water, whence the oil will move by smaller tanker, or by pipeline, to the main distributing centres. If this is to be the pattern the Thames Estuary will still have an important role to play. But flexibility will be needed, flexibility and adaptability. For events are moving so fast that the port which cannot adapt will be left behind as surely as Bruges was left behind whilst its ancient rival Ghent went ahead.

12

The Old Kingsferry Bridge to Sheppey
The New Kingsferry Bridge

17

THE "NETHERLANDISH COMMUNITY"

One of my most vivid memories of childhood is standing on the beach at Southend-on-Sea and watching boatloads of holiday-makers going off to some strange remote island called "Canvey Island". To me it was some mysterious Treasure Island somewhere beyond the horizon. Today, even though I have come to know Canvey Island intimately, it has never lost that element of mystery. The casual visitor might find this difficult to understand, and I agree that on a casual visit the island may not seem impressive. But anyone who knows its fascinating past, and has any sense of history at all, must surely come to share this feeling. There is no more historic place in the whole estuary than Canvey Island.

The visitor has a brief glimpse of the past as soon as he drives on to the island for he must needs pass the Dutch Cottage Museum alongside the only road on to the island from the mainland. This has been established recently in one of the two remaining cottages built by the little colony of Dutch people, called in seventeenth-century documents, perhaps a little contemptuously, the "Netherlandish Community". There is another of these curious cottages in Old Canvey Village. Both of them have thatched roofs, and they were built by the original Dutch settlers in 1618 and 1622. They are double-storeyed, and when the great flood of 1953 drowned almost the whole of Canvey Island these old cottages remained dry. Probably they were built round for greater strength in case of flooding, or did the Dutch share the old superstition that the Devil lurks in corners?

The Dutchmen arrived on Canvey Island as a result of a deal between a wealthy Dutch merchant named Joas Croppenburgh and a number of Englishmen who owned land on the island . . . Canvey at that time was wholly salting marsh, that is, it was covered by water at every high tide, and this was most inconvenient for the thousands of sheep grazing the saltings, not to mention the shepherds who looked after them. Moreover it ruled out any permanent human habitation. Thus a deal was concluded under which the Dutch agreed to build a wall round the island, provided the English landowners gave them one-third of the land so enclosed. In 1622 the wall was built and several hundred Dutch workers and their families took up residence on the island, to farm the land they had earned for themselves.

The story of the conflicts between the Dutch and their English neighbours fill many pages of the *Annals of the Dutch Church in England* (Austin Friars); I have spent many hours in the Guildhall Library studying these old documents and they tell a vivid story of the ceaseless antagonism between the two races on the island. One constant ground for conflict was the water level of the marsh ditches. The Dutch being arable farmers wanted a lower level of water than the English who were mainly livestock farmers and wanted lush pastures. The resentment of the English at the Dutch habit of draining the ditches expressed itself in this piece of contemporary doggerel:

> Why should we stay then and perish with thirst?
> To the New World in the morn then away let us go
> For if the Dutch Colony get there first
> It's a thousand to one they'll drain that too.

Another cause of conflict was the repair and maintenance of the river wall. The Dutchmen, in their original deal, had undertaken to keep the wall they had built in good repair, and in time this responsibility took the form of an annual tax or "scot" on all the "third acre" lands, as they came to be called. The other lands on the island literally went "scot free". Thus the task of looking after the wall fell upon the shoulders of the Dutch people on the island, although the English benefited as much if not more. Naturally the Dutch came to resent this situation, and in times of bad flooding when the walls were breached, the third acre rates alone were inadequate to provide for the effective defence of the island from the sea. Eventually therefore the other lands, called the "freelands", became eligible for wall rates, but at a lower level than the third acre lands. When developers bought up lands on Canvey Island in the early twentieth century they generally avoided the third acre lands and if one compares the distribution of the third acre lands with the built-up areas on the island one finds that they are mutually exclusive almost everywhere.

In due course the Dutch colony came to an end at the beginning of the eighteenth century. Just how this happened we do not know. It seems unlikely that there was a mass exodus back to the Netherlands, but what seems most probable is that the Dutch people had become so anglicized by this time that they decided to abandon their own language (they had received special dispensation from King Charles in 1628 to hold services in their own tongue—another cause of dissension within the community as their English neighbours on the island had to go to South Benfleet, a difficult journey across the marshes, to attend church) and to adopt English ways and English names. In 1712 the old Dutch church was pulled down and a new chapel erected, an English curate arrived, and the community of "Low Country Strangers" (another of the titles by which they were known) was at an end. Only the characteristic round cottages, and the several tongue-twisting Dutch road names on the Island, have survived.

The next century and a half was a period of quiet rural isolation with much agricultural prosperity during the third quarter of the nineteenth century, the so-called Golden Age of British Agriculture. After 1875, however, the prosperity came to an abrupt end with the flow into Britain of wheat from the New World. Corn prices dropped to a level which left virtually no return to the English producer, and hundreds of acres of land on Canvey Island passed out of cultivation. A wilderness of rough untended grassland, weeds and bracken invaded the once-prosperous farm lands, farm buildings deteriorated, farmers and farm workers migrated to other areas and to the cities in search of a livelihood. Into this vacuum came a new influx of people—Londoners from the East End looking for a cheap plot of land for their retirement, or for holiday homes. Estate agents bought up farms for a song, and then attracted potential buyers of individual plots with the offer of a free rail ticket, and a free lunch complete with wine. Many took the bait and found themselves owners of a small parcel of land on Canvey Island, often completely devoid of any public services, and not even a road. Gradually a haphazard collection of holiday shacks and retirement bungalows, a rash of "We'rin"s and "Chez Nous"s, spread over the eastern end of the island, the end nearest to the beaches and furthest from the Old

Dutch Village. Access to the island was by ford at low tide for many years, but in 1931 a bridge was built across to South Benfleet, a bridge which opened to allow small ships to pass through. Although still in use at present this is now obsolete and a new one is planned. The population when the bridge was built was 3,500. Twenty years later it was over 11,000 and today it is nearer 20,000. During the summer season the resident population is swollen by many thousands of holiday visitors.

The great flood of January 31st 1953, although by no means the first in Canvey's history, was the first since the island had been developed residentially. The people were caught totally unprepared for such a disaster. Anyone who is interested can read the enthralling minute-by-minute account of the flood as it hit the coast of Essex, in Hilda Grieve's *The Great Tide*. Her book, a monumental work of nearly 900 painstaking pages, contains many heart-rending stories of the many personal tragedies of that time, of which this is a typical example:

In one bungalow in the Sixty Acres [on Canvey Island] a family with nine children under sixteen years of age awaited rescue. When the water first burst in, the father, standing on the table, had broken a hole in the ceiling, climbed into the rafter space, and lifted seven of the children up, one by one, from the table. Then the table disintegrated. The mother was left standing in the water below, holding the two youngest boys; both of them died in her arms as they waited. About 8 o'clock in the morning a third small boy fell into the water through the hole in the ceiling. An elder brother dived in after him, and stood in five feet of water holding him up, for two hours more. Then, his legs numb, the bigger boy's strength gave out, and he had to let the child go and hang on to the edge of the top of the door for support until a boat came for them.

On Canvey Island alone, fifty-eight people lost their lives and thousands were rendered temporarily homeless. No wonder the opening speaker at a conference called soon afterwards to discuss the floods called them " . . . probably the worst peace-time disaster Great Britain has ever known".

But the story of Canvey Island did not of course end with the 1953 floods. The die had been cast many years before. Canvey could not return now to rural isolation—it was now a large urban area and so it would remain. The only alternative therefore was to heighten the walls so that never again would the island be flooded. During the 1950s sheet steel piling was sunk into the earthen river walls fronting the River Thames to raise them by an additional three feet. Since the 1953 tide was only a foot and a half above previous exceptional tides this should allow an adequate safety margin. Tewkes Creek and Smallgains Creek on the east side of the island were both sealed off to reduce the length of the walls to be maintained. On a recent visit to the island I noticed that many of the new houses built since the floods have two storeys or more—whereas previously most residential building on the island had been bungalows. This may have been due to shortage of land, but it may also reflect an awareness of the dangers of living below high tide level—nearly all the casualties on Canvey Island in 1953 occurred in bungalows. Canvey Island is probably safer now than it has ever been since it was first enclosed.

In one sense Canvey Island is the most up-to-date community in England. I refer to the fact that the island was selected in 1965 by the North Thames Gas Board as the first place in the country where all the gas appliances would be converted for the use of natural gas. By July 1966 the whole island had been converted. Canvey was chosen because it is a self-contained community with a rapidly increasing demand for gas, and also of course because Canvey happens to be the main terminal in Britain for the supply of natural gas from the Sahara. In 1959, when the first cargoes of liquified natural gas came to Canvey Island, there were the same doubts and fears as there had been a century before when the first cargoes of petroleum arrived. Happily there have been no serious explosions or fires, and today two specially built methane carriers, the *Methane Princess* and the *Methane Progress*, together do about sixty round trips a year from the North African coast to Britain with a combined annual delivery of 700,000 tons of liquified gas, representing 10 per cent of this country's total gas consumption. One ship docks at the Canvey Terminal every $5\frac{1}{2}$ days and the cargo is delivered into seven storage tanks with a total storage capacity of 22,000 tons. From Canvey the methane travels by pipeline to Birmingham, Manchester, and Leeds, along a specially constructed grid 350 miles long.

Today Canvey Island is a flourishing Urban District with a growing recreation industry, a new oil refinery, and soon a new bridge to the mainland. It is sometimes called, after Southend-on-Sea, London's "Second Lung". Canvey has indeed travelled a long way since it was described only a little over half a century ago as "the loneliest place in the Home Counties".

18

THE FOUR "S's":
SOUTHEND, SHOEBURYNESS, SHEERNESS AND SHEPPEY

The problem of where the river ends and the sea begins may seem a purely academic one, but it is not. It is a matter of considerable importance. For many centuries, however, the issue did not cause any concern since it had been settled as far back as the time of Richard I, that the line should be drawn between the Crowstone, placed on the foreshore at Chalkwell near Southend-on-Sea, and the London Stone by the entrance to the Yantlet Channel. Richard I had made a bargain with the City of London whereby the London Mayor was made the Conservator of the River Thames in exchange for a loan from the City to finance one of his crusades. The line between the Crowstone and the London Stone was drawn up to indicate the eastward extent of the City's jurisdiction. The present Crowstone dates from 1836; its predecessor, which dated from 1755, may still be seen in the grounds of Prittlewell Priory, the South-east Essex Museum, to whom it was presented by the P.L.A. in 1952.

When the Port of London Authority was established the seaward limit of the River Thames was fixed along an imaginary line drawn between Havengore Creek in Essex and Warden Point in Kent. This limit had already been fixed, for Customs purposes, in 1883. However, as the size of vessels continued to increase, especially in recent years with the developments of the super-tankers, the P.L.A. became more and more concerned with navigation problems beyond their seaward limit. In 1964 the changed circumstances were officially recognized by the "Port of London (Extension of Seaward Limit) Act" which gave the P.L.A. powers to extend its seaward limit another twenty-two miles to a line drawn between Gunfleet Old Lighthouse and the

North Foreland. This passes near the Tongue Lightvessel and so the name "Tongue" has been adopted for convenience as the seaward limit, just as the "Nore" was used for the old seaward limit. This is more than just a paper change. Already the P.L.A. have announced a plan to dredge the main approach channels, and as far up-river as the Thameshaven oil jetties, to provide a minimum depth of water of 48 feet at high tide.

I still find it difficult to think of the estuary between the Nore and the Tongue as part of the River Thames. After all, the river is already six miles wide at the Nore; at the Tongue it is several times wider still. This wide expanse of water is broken only by the lightvessels, such as the Barrow Deep and the Mid Barrow and the Tongue itself, and by the rusting remains of the old war-time forts such as the Shivering Sands Tower slap in the middle of the estuary. This one at least is put to a useful purpose as the P.L.A. have their most easterly tide gauge here and the tide level is radioed at regular intervals to the Thames Navigation Service Headquarters at Gravesend, as they are from the other gauges at Southend Pier and Tilbury. There is nothing to distinguish river from sea when the shore line recedes out of sight, but we must move with the times and realize that the configuration of the sea bed is today far more vital than the shape of the coastline. So we must now regard the four "S's" as forming an integral part of the Thames Estuary.

Southend-on-Sea, the largest town on the Thames Estuary, is almost entirely a product of the last two centuries. Before about 1700 there was as little at Southend as there was at Brighton, its sister resort on the South Coast; both were small fishing communities located down on the foreshore where the boats were beached. The cliffs at Southend and the thickly wooded plateau lands behind were at that time completely undeveloped. The community lived mainly by oyster cultivation, the whole foreshore between Shoebury and Hadleigh being devoted to oyster beds. This industry began as the result of an accidental discovery by a Southchurch man named Outing. He had been out in a boat gathering native oysters, and had thrown some of the smaller ones on to the foreshore. A year later he returned to the same spot and noticed that these oysters had much improved in size and quality. This gave him the idea of cultivating oysters so he promptly acquired a lease of the foreshore and set up the industry

which was worth tens of thousands of pounds by the end of the
eighteenth century.

Southend-on-Sea and Leigh nearby continued to have an oyster
fishery until the early twentieth century when it was killed by
pollution in the river. Since then only the shellfish and shrimping
industries have survived, mostly at Leigh. For some curious reason
oysters are not usually regarded as shellfish, which term is reserved
for such creatures as cockles, mussels and whelks. The landings of
cockles at Leigh are double those of any other area, whilst Leigh
accounts for the great majority of the shrimps caught in the
Thames Estuary. The old oyster beds are now mainly used for the
more humble winkles.

Long before the oyster industry had died another, and ultimately far more important, industry had been born at Southend.
In the 1790s it was decided to develop Southend as a watering
place. The cliff top was cleared of woodland and the Royal
Terrace and Royal Hotel (they acquired the title "Royal" after
the visits of the Princess of Wales in 1801 and 1803) were built.
The Old Town has easy access to the foreshore, but for this new
resort town fine views were more important than easy access—
so a new road had to be built up the steep cliffside to the plateau.
For a while the new watering place was very fashionable, and
Jane Austen referred to it in some of her novels. The first pier
was built in 1829 and many of the town's visitors arrived on the
newly introduced steamers. The present pier, the longest in the
world, was built in 1889 and has been extended since. However,
the steamships also had other ports of call such as Gravesend and
Margate and these also became popular watering places, so that
Southend did not show any remarkable growth. One suspects,
also, that the climate, and particularly the ague which was still
very prevalent in the neighbourhood, may have deterred visitors.
The arrival of the railway in 1856, and the building of the new
town a few years later, gave a fillip to the town's development
but still its growth was slow. The really phenomenal growth
came in the twentieth century, from 29,000 in 1901 to about
175,000 today. The town has long been popular with Londoners
out for the day and has earned a reputation as a rather unfashionable place because of these "day-trippers". Those who visit the
town for the first time are therefore often surprised to find how
attractive it is, and how far removed from its popular image.

The little seaport of Leigh, which has now grown into the large residential suburb of Southend: "Leigh-on-Sea" has had an intriguing history. In Tudor times the port was the ninth largest in England with 1,900 tons of shipping to its credit. At about this time also the town's shipbuilding industry reached its peak. Admiral Blake refitted his fleet here in 1653. However, by 1800 the town had shrunk to a village and the people were, to quote an official document of the time, "mainly smugglers or wreckers". The town developed some importance as a centre of the shellfish industry, and the boiling sheds on the foreshore with their mounds of cockle shells lying around, together with the fleet of Bawleys and other fishing vessels, still attract many visitors. These apart there is little left to remind the visitor that Leigh was a major port when its upstart neighbour Southend was not even a name on the map (it is in fact the "south end" of the parish of Prittle-well).

Like Leigh, Shoeburyness is another historic site which was once more important than Southend, although it too is completely overshadowed by its larger neighbour. Projecting as it does into the estuary of the Thames, Shoeburyness, with South-church its neighbour, was a place of considerable importance in the days when ships were of shallow draught and the lack of deep water was no great inconvenience. The East Saxons settled in this corner of Essex in large numbers, as witness the number of villages ending in "ing", and the Scandinavian invaders used Shoebury as their base for the invasion of the Rochford Hundred. Shoebury is now best known for the presence there of the army's weapon testing establishment. Guns are fired in the direction of the Maplin Sands, off Foulness Island, where the shells can be recovered from the hard sands at ebb tide. The Maplin Sands are uniquely suited for this purpose, which is perhaps unfortunate as some people have suggested Foulness as being a suitable site for London's third airport.

The Isle of Sheppey (or strictly speaking just "Sheppey" since the suffix "ey", as in "Canvey", signifies an island, i.e. the Isle of Sheep) has about half its area above high tide level. Indeed it presents to the River Thames quite an imposing cliff, the low land being mostly along the southern side of the island by the River Swale. Perhaps "cliff" is not quite the right word for this extended area of landslips from Sheerness to Warden Point, a geologist's dream, but if they are not sheer they are certainly high. At Minster the London Clay backbone of the island rises several hundred feet above the flat marsh; long flights of steps lead down from the church to the village clustered below it. Like Shoebury on the opposite shore the Isle of Sheppey occupies a position of great strategic importance in the estuary. He who controls Sheppey controls the Medway, and can threaten the Thames and the Essex shore. The Danes, for instance, used Sheppey as their main base for their attack on Essex, and when they were defeated at Benfleet they retreated to Shoebury where their fleet lay ready and sailed back across the estuary to Sheppey. Because of its key position, Edward III decided to place an important castle on Sheppey, and he chose Queenborough as the site because it commanded the Swale as well as the Medway. In those days of smaller vessels the Swale was an important channel. Even today it is used by ocean-going vessels bringing raw materials to the paper mills at Kemsley. Queenborough used to be called King-borough, but Edward changed its name in honour of his queen. Queenborough Castle was demolished by Cromwell, and so was not even in existence to deter the Dutch fleet when it sailed up the Medway in 1667. Today Queenborough has an air of faded glory. The main street in particular is remarkably wide, and runs back at right angles from the Medway—but its main characteristic is its quietness. I have never seen such a quiet main street of any town. Perhaps all the activity is centred on the Creek which runs behind the main street and is crowded with small craft.

To replace Queenborough, Sheerness had been designated as the site for a new dock and fort, and between 1665 and 1667 Pepys makes several references in his diaries to visits he made to inspect the works in progress there. But when De Ruyter sailed up the Medway the fort was only half finished. It was quickly silenced by the Dutch, who landed and gained possession of the fort, whilst the Dutch fleet continued on its way up the Med-way, broke the chain that had been thrown across the river, crushed the weak resistance of Upnor Castle, and proceeded to destroy eight great ships lying at anchor, capturing the finest of them all, the *Royal Charles*. It is not an episode in our history that any Englishman can remember with pride, any more than we do the Mutiny of the Nore in 1797. It was at Sheerness that the leader of the mutineers, a seaman named Parker, paraded insolently through the streets and threatened that if his plans were interfered with the town would be blown to bits. However, there were bitter internecine quarrels between the rebel leaders, and when the Trinity House Brethren removed the buoys and sea markers in the Outer Estuary so that the ships could not sail out the mutiny collapsed and the rebellious ships sailed into Sheerness one after the other. Despite these humiliations, however, the dockyard at Sheerness did useful service for nearly three hundred years.

Sheerness is not an easy harbour to enter because of the race of the Medway through the narrow channel between the Isle of Grain and Sheppey. I remember some years ago my brother took his minesweeper into the dockyard there and we had to make more than one approach run before we could get through the narrow dock entrance safely. On that occasion my brother was paying off his ship. We little realized then that within a few years the whole dockyard itself would be paid off. The Navy abandoned Sheerness Dockyard in 1960 because it had become superfluous to their requirements. Since then there has been a period of some uncertainty on the island as to what its economic future might be. However, there has been considerable growth of private industry, particularly at Sheerness, the only town of any size (15,000 people), whilst communications with the mainland have been vastly improved by the building of the new Kingsferry Bridge over the Swale, the only road and rail link to the mainland. I crossed the old bridge several times and what a ramshackle affair it was. The bridge was constantly being hit by ships trying to negotiate its narrow passage in the awkward wind conditions of the exposed Swale channel, and on such occasions, the 30,000 people on the island were completely cut off. Emergency supplies of milk and other necessary foodstuffs had to be arranged, and ferry services instituted to carry the thousands of workers to and from the island. In 1956 this happened three times in three months, and on one occasion the bridge was out of action for a whole week. It got to the point where a national newspaper sent down a reporter to do a story on the beleaguered island. He first went to see the bridge with its drawbridge stuck eighty feet in the air "like a great reptile jaw" and then did a tour of the island. "Sheppey has a desolate forgotten look", he reported, "and seems

immensely distant from the centre of things . . . everyone blames
it on 'The Bridge'." The following year it was decided to build
a new bridge, and this was opened in 1960. Its four pillars, each
100 feet high, which enable the road and rail bridge to be lifted
vertically, dominate the lowlands of the Swale for many miles
around. To the people of Sheppey they are an assurance that they
are not forgotten, and today if people on the island talk about
"the bridge" it is with pride not despair.

In the last few years Sheerness Harbour has begun a new life as
a commercial port, and it has even been improved to take ships
450 feet long and drawing 25 feet of water. In common with
Dover, Ramsgate, Felixstowe and other small ports on the East
and South coasts, Sheerness has benefited from the rapid growth
in trade with Europe, and from the tendency to use small ports
to avoid the labour restrictions and stoppages so characteristic of
the main ports. It lies outside the jurisdiction of the P.L.A. and
therefore escapes heavy docking charges. Commercial cargoes
have increased from 20,000 tons per annum in 1961–2 to 250,000
tons today, whilst the port now handles over 1,000 ships a year.
It is curious to see lines of imported Skoda cars outside the granite
walls of the old dockyard, or commercial vehicles trundling
through the old dock gates, and past the old figureheads that are
to be found at the entrance to every naval dockyard, laden with
champagne or sherry or fruit, vegetables or animal foods. With
Sheerness, the Medway group of ports is now the fifth largest in
Britain in terms of tonnage.

Another asset of Sheerness, which is not always realized, is its
fine position fronting the River Thames. The town has an excellent promenade which terminates at the foothills of the cliffs of
Minster, and is a holiday town of considerable importance. The
fact that Sheerness is no longer a naval harbour may help the
resort industry develop a more attractive image for the town.
Sheerness is well set on its new course; what of the rest of Sheppey?
There are rumours of massive developments in Sheppey, including the possibility of the marshes being used for London's third
airport. The town and Country Planning Association recently
published a plan proposing increased industrial and residential
development in the Thames Estuary linked to a Thameside airport (in substitution for Stanstead), together with a bridge across
the estuary carrying a motorway linking East Anglia with the

Channel Tunnel. It may sound revolutionary, but it is thinking on this scale that is needed to meet the problems, and the potentialities, of an area like the Thames Estuary. More immediately, however, the most likely major development on Sheppey is a big expansion of water-based recreation using the wonderful opportunities of the Swale and Lower Medway.

Of the villages in the interior of Sheppey, some are very old and remote such as Elmley and Harty. Harty, in particular, must be among the most unfrequented of villages within an hour's drive of London. To reach it one has to travel 4½ miles from Eastchurch across the wide open marshes of Sheppey, with thousands of sheep grazing the lush pastures as they have done since the island first received its name, up the little hill on which the village stands, through a gate across the road, and you are there—at Harty church which to all intents and purposes *is* Harty village. The church smells old, it literally reeks of the twelfth century (when services are on it must reek of oil to judge by the oil lamps in the pews), and it has a fine parish chest with medieval carvings. The grass is long, gravestones are few (there are few people to die here), and the wind never stops blowing. You have to be hale at Harty. On the journey back, along the only road, we see signs of a new industry—the marshes are being cultivated for turf to decorate town gardens.

But the most interesting by far of all the villages of Sheppey is Minster, or as it has come to be called recently, Minster-on-Sea. It is now only half a mile from the coast, although at one time, before erosion took its toll, it was in the middle of the island. Here is located one of the oldest churches in England—the Abbey founded by Queen Sexburga in A.D. 670. She must have been a very saintly woman for according to a medieval document in the British Museum " . . . no one was more temperate than she in the pursuit of pleasure, no one humbler in the face of royal pride, no one more unassuming in spirit". Life must have been relatively peaceful on the Isle of Sheppey at this time, but violent days lay ahead. In 832, says the *Anglo Saxon Chronicle*, 'the heathen men overran the Isle of Sheppey". They brought with them rape, pillage and bloodshed. For the next 200 years the peaceful Isle of Sheppey, with its fine views of the Thames, Medway and Swale, became one vast armed camp, and at times a bloody battlefield. The Abbey was destroyed by fire (confirmed by the discovery of fire-damaged stonework during the nineteenth-century restoration work) and the inmates were put to death, even the nuns. Not that such violence was the exclusive preserve of the Danes. Violence breeds violence; there are several churches in the district where the doors are said to have been covered with the skins of Danes. Alfred the Great, Haesten, Godwin and Harold are some of the people who figure prominently in the history of this troublous period. The rebuilding of the Minster took place in the twelfth century, with Kentish ragstone and some Caen stone brought over from Normandy, as was done for Canterbury Cathedral. The tower was never completed, although it was planned on a grand scale so that the church today has a curiously unbalanced appearance, the massive base of the tower seeming altogether out of proportion to the stubby little belfry on top. The old gate house, massive like the base of the tower, is all that remains today of the old monastic foundation.

We continue our journey along the main road of Sheppey, virtually its only road, from Minster along to its eastern extremity at Leysdown. This village has developed remarkably in recent years as a holiday resort of a rather garish kind. It has everything the day-tripper, camper or caravanner might need, including Parrish's Casino, Greeno's Fish Bar and a large amusement arcade called "The Golden Horseshoe". In the vicinity are some of the largest caravan parks in South-east England. When I was last there it was after the 1953 floods and the place was just getting its second breath, the sea wall was being rebuilt and the flood devastation was being cleaned up. But all this is now a dim and distant memory. Leysdown is firmly set on its career of catering for the needs of an increasingly motorized and leisured population.

We will not grudge them their amusements, but let us not end our long journey here. Rather let us return to Eastchurch and take the other, or northern, road to Warden Point, for many years the southern end of the seaward limit of the Port of London. From here an imaginary line runs eastwards for another twenty-two miles and then turns northwards through the Tongue to Gunfleet Old Lighthouse, and so back to Havengore Creek—it now takes three imaginary lines to mark the seaward limit of the Port of London whereas it only used to take one. The road to Warden Point, like so many we have encountered in these pages, wanders in a lazy fashion towards the sea and then just stops dead at a line

Minster Church, Isle of Sheppey
Old Dutch Cottage, Canvey Island

of railings. Here the heavily eroded cliff drops steeply away to the river hundreds of feet below. A few yards away to the north is the coastguard look-out tower, not an attractive building in any way but it looks out towards the Tongue and it symbolizes for us the last milestone on our journey—the rest is sea. We have travelled seventy-five miles from Teddington and fifty-seven from London Bridge. Now as we gaze out towards the open estuary of the Thames we cannot help wondering what the future will hold. Will London follow the precedent set by Rotterdam and build an entirely new port out there in the mouth of the river—one capable of docking many of the larger ships now coming into service? Considering the transformation that we have witnessed in the estuary in the last ten years who can say what the next twenty-five years will bring? That is what is so fascinating about the Thames. It is, in John Burns's well-known phrase, "liquid history", but it is also history in the making. In the waters of this river have been mirrored every major event in the history of these islands, and it is so still. Its tidal heart-beat is the heart-beat of a nation. In a very real sense, the story of the River Thames, past, present and future, is the story of England as a whole.

Town Square, Corringham New Town
The Lobster Smack, Canvey Island

19

POSTSCRIPT

THE THAMES IN A.D. 2000—
A VISION OF THE FUTURE

As our hovercraft skims past Petersham Ait, under old Richmond
Bridge, and along the beautiful Syon Reach, we see a Thames
hardly changed from what it was thirty years ago. But as we
approach Brentford Dock (it still keeps the old name although
the dock went out of use years ago) we see signs of major new
developments. The river becomes busy with yachts and pleasure
craft of all kinds, and as we pass under the graceful new footbridge
linking Brentford with Kew Gardens, we see where they have
been coming from—the new yachting basin and marina occupying the whole of the space between the shore and Brentford Ait.
It is difficult to believe that these fine riverside homes, ten storeys
high and sloping backwards so that each flat has a riverside
terrace, and the beautifully landscaped marina they overlook,
were once the site of a muddy backwater fringed with derelict
industrial wharves, run-down factories and the old gas works.
But of course that was back in the 'sixties, before the barrage was
built at Woolwich. In those days the mud was exposed at every
tide; it is astonishing to think that the people put up with it for
so long. What a waste of the river—just to think that along the
whole of this mile-long stretch the people of Brentford had no
access to their river at all. Where Brentford Dock used to be there
is now a new town, and immensely popular it is too because the
old canal provides ready access to the river and people can float
their boats down to the tideway from their own back gardens
instead of having to haul them to the launching ramps.

Yachting basins and marinas are indeed a common sight as we

continue our journey down the river, one of the biggest being at Barnes where the Beverley Brook joins the Thames. At Nine Elms the Covent Garden Market (it has also retained its old name) attracts river traffic like bees to a honey pot; there is as much up-river traffic as there used to be in spite of the barrage—in fact if anything there is more because the congestion on the roads has forced more short-distance traffic on to the river. Wandsworth Gas Works is still there, but no longer does the coal come by sea as it did once, it now comes by pipeline from the great coal wharves at Erith below the barrage—just like the sewage but in the opposite direction! All the oil used for the gas works above the barrage comes by pipeline direct from the oil terminals at Thamesmouth in the outer estuary, and the older refineries at the Isle of Grain and Thameshaven.

We come now to Kings Reach, still the show-piece of London River as it has always been. Here are the imposing new buildings like the new National Theatre below Waterloo Bridge, and St Thomas's Hospital. The Houses of Parliament are still there, but after a decade of fierce argument they have at last decided to move Parliament to the government campus now well established at Windsor; ministers were getting tired of commuting between their departments and Westminster. The old Parliament building will be a Museum of the British People. But it is the bridges of Kings Reach that best symbolize the London of the twenty-first century; a London that seems to have suddenly rediscovered its river. Instead of the ugly old railway bridge at Hungerford there is now an exciting concoction of restaurants, viewing platforms and even art galleries, gracing the wide new footbridge across to the Southbank Cultural Centre. London Bridge has just had a pedestrian deck built over the roadway and some say that similar developments will take place there too. Maybe London Bridge will replace Tower Bridge (still there but with its bascules permanently raised these days) as the symbol of London. There are fine new embankments too. On the south side, the Albert Embankment now runs right along the Southwark bank to London Bridge, where Southwark Cathedral can breathe again with its fine open frontage to the river—it provides an aspect worthy of the new London Bridge. On the north bank a new embankment continues the Victorian Embankment past the site of the old Mermaid Theatre (they have found it a new home nearby) to London Bridge, and Upper Thames Street is now one of the best addresses in London because there are marinas all along here and these are not allowed in Kings Reach. There are some ultra-modern flats overlooking the river, whilst here and there one of the old warehouses has been converted into a hotel or public hall, just to remind us what this stretch of riverside once looked like. Wren would approve of it as it is now—this is almost what he wanted to do 350 years ago.

In the river itself there are several floating swimming pools, like the original one built twenty-five years ago off Charing Cross, and there is a floating helicopter station off the new Albert Embankment. The river is used for recreation much more now than it used to be, and because of the increasing number of yachts and other shipping using the river it has become necessary to consider allocating particular periods of the day specifically for pleasure boating (water-skiing having a short half-hour to itself), and others for the exclusive use of hovercraft. All this is the responsibility of the new Thames Valley Authority (Britain's own T.V.A. Scheme for the comprehensive development of the river and its banks).

As we move into what used to be called Dockland, we see an altogether new London; a kind of Venetian city in miniature. Places like St Katharines, Shadwell and Wapping Marina, are very attractive residential areas where there is more water than land. It is strange to think that only fifty years ago these areas were avoided for residential purposes because the winds drove the smoke over towards the East End—and because the waterside was needed for commercial shipping. Now there are no coal fires, and little commercial shipping of the old type . . . whilst people now seek the water above all—the water and the wind for sailing. Nearly everyone in Wapping has his own boat. Because the docks occupied large areas, when they were redeveloped it was possible to design large new estates so that whole districts changed character almost overnight.

Other Wapping-like developments are taking place further down-river at such places as Rotherhithe, where part of the old Surrey Docks are being re-developed, East India Dock and the old Millwall Docks.

The secret of London's "New Venice" is the great Thames Barrage which we are now approaching at Woolwich. This huge complex of dams and locks and hovercraft ramps protects the City of London from the effects of the tide and maintains permanent high water above Woolwich. It was only after the terrible floods of 1985, far worse than those of 1953, that the decision was taken to build the Barrage, and since then the flood danger to London has been completely removed. Vessels pass through the several locks provided in the Scheme, but the number of large vessels using the upper river has much declined since the 'sixties and now that London Port is completely containerized it is mainly small lighters and coasters that use the river above the barrage. The barrage was cunningly sited just above the entrance to the Royal Docks so that if there is pressure on the locks in the river vessels can pass right through the Royal Docks by-passing the barrage. Our hovercraft, of course, is independent of locks—we simply pass over the ramp provided.

Immediately beyond the barrage on our right we pass Thamesmead, now twenty years old, but still renowned in Britain as the first of the new-look "water-towns". It has a slightly period appearance now, with its low river frontage and industrialized building; whilst the recent raising of the river wall as a result of the barrage (the town lies below the barrage and is therefore not protected by it) has somewhat damaged the scale of the town's riverside development. Nevertheless Thamesmead proved what could be done to integrate water recreation as part of everyday living and it has an honoured place in Thameside history.

In the 1960s the stretch of river we are now entering, between Barking and Tilbury, was only half-developed; it was a kind of industrial wilderness between the port proper and its outlier at Tilbury. But today the river "below the barrage" has completely outgrown old Dockland in importance. The reason, in a word, is containerization. Ships can be turned round now in only one-fifth of the time it took in the old-fashioned way. Tilbury, in particular, has grown to be the largest container-port in Britain and one of the largest in the world. Below Tilbury the Port of London continues along both banks of the river in an unbroken line of oil installations, grain jetties and mills, container-docks and passenger terminals. This is *Great Expectations* country, but Charles Dickens surely never expected anything like this! A tunnel crosses the river at Gravesend and carries the great auto-hoverway linking the Channel Tunnel with the Midlands and North; this is now the biggest traffic artery in the country, and it completely by-passes London.

As our hovercraft speeds towards the outer estuary, passing several of the 200,000-ton oil tankers that now reach Thameshaven along the newly dredged 54 feet channel, we begin to see signs of the greatest of all the new projects on London River—Thames-mouth. This is a great new deep water harbour being built in the outer estuary. A breakwater of mammoth proportions is being built out into the estuary between Foulness and the North Kent Coast. Behind this will be built London's new port on reclaimed land, together with a new airport, London's fifth major airport. Who would have guessed, back in 1965 when the Seaward Limit of the Port of London was moved twenty-two miles out to sea, that within thirty-five years the Port would almost have caught up with its Seaward Limit!

All this is a vision of the future—but it is not a fantasy. Every one of the changes described above has either been already planned, or has been put forward as a serious proposition. The containerization of the port and the industrialization of the lower river are already happening; the release of the upper river for recreation is still largely a hope. If the vision is not to turn into a nightmare we must ensure that the youngsters who will be seeing in the New Year in A.D. 2000, will know a River Thames that gives as much pleasure above the barrage as it gives profit below it; a river in which it is the rule, not the exception, to fish, swim, sail and water-ski; a river beside which it is a sought-after privilege to live; in short a river that, in the words of Sir Patrick Aber-crombie, "presents unequalled opportunities for public enjoy-ment, civic splendour and residential amenity".

INDEX

A

Abbey Mills, 49
Abercrombie, Sir Patrick, 41, 199
Adelaide House, 35
Adelphi Terrace, 46–7
Albert Bridge, 39
Albert Embankment, 49, 51, 83, 196, 197
Alfred the Great, 108, 192
Allhallows, 145, 149, 155, 162–5, 168, 175
Alpha Cement Company, 155
Anglo-Iranian Oil Company, 168
Anglo-Saxon *Chronicle*, 28, 191

B

Bankside, 66, 76, 79, 82
Barber, Thomas W., 52
Barking, 123–5, 198
Barking Outfall, 49, 75, 118–19, 123
Barnes, 41, 196
Barrow Deep, 185
Barry, Charles, 48, 78–9, 82
Basildon, 175
Bata Shoe Factory, 160
Battersea, 35, 40, 62, 65, 68, 82
Bawley Bay, 135–6, 187
Bazalgette, Sir Jos., 40, 49–51, 84, 119
Beckton Gas Works, 123
Bede, Venerable, 28
Belgic People, 16–17
Bells Hard, 164
Bermondsey, 65, 103, 109, 118
Beverley Brook, 196
Bevin, Ernest, 117
Bicknors, 135
Big Ben, 78, 83
Billingsgate, 18–19, 31, 57, 91, 98, 102, 123, 171

Bill Meroy's Creek, 152
Bird, Professor, 98–9
Black Deep, 119
Blackfriars, 18, 35, 38, 40, 46–7, 51, 66, 69, 75, 81
Blackheath, 109
Blackwall, 37, 92, 103, 111–16, 132
Blake, Admiral, 187
Blyth Sands, 149, 163, 176
Boadicea, Queen, 85
Boat Race, 63, 74
Bowaters Paper Mill, 132
Bow Creek, 115
Brentford, 61, 195
British Dredging (London) Co., 104
Broadness Point, 132
Brunel, 36, 40, 84, 103, 107
Brunswick Dock, 93, 112
Brunswick Generating Station, 112
Bugsby's Reach, 102, 115, 120
Burghers of Calais, 86
Burns, John, 117, 193
Bywell Castle, 122

C

Caesar, Julius, 16–17
Camberwell, 105
Canaletto, 65, 70, 81
Cannon Street, 17–18, 41, 55, 61, 73, 82
Canvey Island, 12, 145–9, 174–83, 187
Carlyle, 84
Carr, Frank, 111, 115
Casson, Sir Hugh, 61
Cattle Plague, 172
Chadwell St. Mary, 139
Chalk, 159
Chalkwell, 184

Channel Tunnel, 191, 198
Chapman & Andree, 138
Charing Cross, 16, 40, 47, 50, 63, 81, 83, 197
Charles I, 180
Charles II, 33, 71, 109, 110, 140
Chaucer, 65, 80
Chelsea, 32, 39–41, 49, 50, 61, 67–8, 76, 84, 110
Cherry Garden Pier, 38, 56, 65, 103
Chichester, Sir Francis, 38, 108, 111
Chinatown, 104
Chiswick, 40, 65
Chrysanthemum, H.M.S., 16, 86
City Canal, 95, 107
Cleopatra's Needle, 84, 86
Cliffe, 129, 130, 145, 155–8, 168
Clovesho, Synod of, 157
Coalhouse Point, 152, 155, 159
Coastguard Service, 168
Cobham, Lord, 164
Colechurch, Peter of, 58
Colemouth Creek, 168
Collier Signal Station, 152
Colquhuon, Dr. Patrick, 95
Comport Family, 163
Conrad, Joseph, 145
Cook, 21
Cooling, 163–4
Cornhill, 16–17, 19
Corringham, 123, 158, 173, 175
Corringham New Town, 175
Cory Bros., 173
Coryton, 145, 173–4
County Hall, 40, 50, 62, 77, 83–4
Covent Garden Market, 196
Crayford, 125, 130
Cremorne Pleasure Gardens, 68, 127
Cromwell, 188
Croppenburg, Joas, 178
Crossness Outfall, 49, 75, 118–19
Crowstone, 184
Cubitt, Thomas, 68
Cubitt Town, 113
Cuckold's Point, 104
Curtiss & Harvey, 156, 173
Customs, H.M., 99, 137
Customs House, 79–80

Cutler Street, 112
Cutty Sark, 110, 111, 115, 131

D

Dagenham, 75, 125–8
Dance, George, 37
Danes, The, 28
Daniell, William, 95
Darent, River, 131
Darnley, Lord, 156
Dartford, 62, 125, 131
Dartford-Purfleet Tunnel, 37, 113, 128, 130, 134
Defoe, Daniel, 85, 123, 147, 159, 160
Denton, 152, 154, 168
Denton Isolation Hospital, 137
Deptford, 49, 92, 104–10, 115
Deptford Foreign Cattle Market, 108, 120, 172
De Ruyter, Admiral, 138, 149, 154, 188
Dickens, Charles, 150, 158, 163, 198
Discovery, 16, 86, 111
Dockland, 36, 102, 113, 197, 198
Dodd, Ralph, 152–4
Doggett's Coat and Badge Race, 74
Doves, The, 76
Dowgate, 17–19, 86
Drake, Sir Francis, 21, 108
Dugdale, William, 44
Durham House, 81

E

Eagle Steamers, 71
Eastchurch, 191
Eastern Dock, 101
East India Company, 92, 108, 112
East India Dock, 96, 107, 112, 140, 197
East Indiamen, 116, 132
East Tilbury, 12, 129, 139, 152, 154, 159–60, 168
Edgware Road, 15, 19
Edward the Confessor, 19, 79